MY AFRICAN ICONS

• Great People in Black History •

MR. IMHOTEP

⭑DEDICATION⭑

To you young King or Queen, ready to discover your true self and the potential you hold within.

To our ancestors,
we will celebrate your memory.

To my father,
for always believing in me.

To Les Brown.
It was hard, but we did it hard.

To the memory of Dr. Llaila Afrika.
For everything you have done for us.

To the memory of Cheikh Anta Diop.
Thank you for the legacy!

Mr. Imhotep

★ CONTENTS ★

INTRODUCTION 05

GODDESS AÏSSATA 14

IEMHETEPU 20

AMANI-HETEPU III 26

EMPRESS TIYE 32

KHUENATEN 36

KING PA ANKHY 42

KANDAKE AMANIRENAS 48

GUDIT 54

YUSUF BEN TACHFIN 60

MANSA MUSA 66

QUEEN AMINA 72

NZINGA MBANDE 76

CHANGAMIRE DOMBO 82

QUEEN NANDI 88

RANAVALONA I 94

MISAKI MIA NIMI 100

FURTHER READINGS 108

ACKNOWLEDGEMENT 109

ABOUT THE AUTHOR 110

YOUR GOAL 112

INTRODUCTION

Writing a book has always been on my mind. I did not know how I was going to accomplish it, what it would be about, or when I would do it, but I had this conviction that at some point, it would happen.

In 2017, I felt the desire to start something new. Something that was not related to anything I had done before. And to be 100% honest with you, I got many choices. I could have pursued a career in many fields. But something happened. I felt that Africa called me. I started to question myself. Looking for answers about my roots. And through that process, I discovered African history. I was coming from a totally different educational background and I did not even know that it was possible to actually study African history in college.

Like most people, I thought that Africa had no interesting history. I had heard about colonial history and a little bit of precolonial history though. But it was mainly the period right before colonization and for the most part, focused on the slave trade. And the way it was introduced to me did not reflect any greatness for Africa. So, in my mind, Africa was that continent that had always been behind in most aspects. It was a place where nothing great ever happened. But through time, I discovered another side of African history. What really happened and how everything started. I actually stumbled upon that because I was questioning myself about the origins of humanity. From the beginning, I started to notice that something did not make sense in what we were taught about Africa. During that period, I started unconsciously to gather pieces of information found in books, documentaries and videos about these topics in my computer for almost a decade.

I discovered the outcasted African scholars like Cheikh Anta Diop, and their work put me in a situation where, for the first time, I had to question the mainstream narrative of African history. The narrative of who I actually was. It was not easy because we use to trust anyone who is white more than any black man, no matter his training (diploma). So, it was difficult to fully believe what the African scholars wrote since they were also labelled as ''Afrocentrists.'' A word used to marginalize them and make them look like some conspiracy theorists. And no one wants to be the one who has been tricked by those weird people… That's how society works.

But because I started to see glitches, I decided to look further and look for the truth. I decided not to choose any side. All I wanted was the truth. And that's how I ended up on this journey.

While on this journey, I started to notice that something was lacking. I was looking for information all over the internet, but most of the sources were only sharing biased information. I discovered that Wikipedia was controlled by a group of people who were doing everything to maintain the lies about Africa. They were writing our history, thus had control over our reality. There was a huge gap between what I had discovered and what was published. It intrigued me. I could not understand why African history was not properly taught. I decided to contact some of the most influential people who possessed platforms about African history that I knew. But none of them considered my opinion.

I thought about giving up, but that itch was too strong. I had the feeling that I would never be happy if I could not share what I had discovered with the world. And that's how Mr. Imhotep was born. From rejections, solitude, but also from love for myself especially love for the people. I did not know how or where to start but I started. The purpose was to bring something new to the table, some fresh air. To share the precolonial history of Africa starting from the dawn of times.

Why that period (precolonial or Imperial Africa) you may ask?

If you've been part of our early journey on social media, you probably already know the answer. But if you don't, here it is:
Because that's the last time Africans, all over the world, were truly themselves.

What does it mean?

As people of African origin, we've been through a lot of hardships. And those events created a trauma that we inherited from our ancestors. That trauma resulted in diverse symptoms like self-hatred, self-sabotaging, etc.

That trauma is a lie that we believe. We think that we are living but our reality is just the result of an invisible trauma. What we consider normal is actually an unhealthy reality.

And history has been highly used to reinforce that trauma within our lives. We've been taught lies about ourselves, about our origins, and our ancestors.

The African American historian Runoko Rashidi once said:
"The worst crime is to teach a child that his history started with slavery."

Unfortunately, that's what most of us have been taught. For years, we've believed that our history started with slavery and colonization. That Kemet (ancient Egypt) was a "Middle Eastern" civilization and had nothing to do with the "primitive blacks living in Sub-Saharan Africa." That the greatest accomplishments had been done by European civilizations, who ended up civilizing the whole world. That Africans started to exist when European explorers discovered them. The list goes on... We've been lied to.

They lied to our grandparents. Which means that our grandparents lied to our parents. Who ended up lying to us. And if we don't break that cycle, we will end up lying to our children. And generations of passing down lies are why we are still suffering. The time is now to heal that trauma.

And the most effective way to achieve that is through education. By educating ourselves about our true history, and then, teaching that truth to our children. Showing them who they really are and not who this Neo colonial system wants them to be.

The Nigerian writer, Chimamanda Ngozi Adichie once said:
"Stories can be used to destroy, but stories can also be used to repair."

I remember the first time I heard that, it touched my soul. Especially because those words explained exactly why I had decided to work in this field. To me, African History could heal the world. That's what we need. I was not really interested in teaching history for the sake of it. What mattered to me was to help the people heal their trauma through history. Because it healed me. And I knew it could heal others too. That's also why I decided to write this book after years of creating content for Mr. Imhotep.
African history has been destroyed, distorted, and hidden. And only the lies are available now. All the tools we use to learn our history have been shaped through a colonial mindset, making them irrelevant to the teaching and the effective HEALING of the people.

We lack effective tools that can truly show us the true beauty and greatness of our African heritage. Tools that will nurture self-love within us. Tools that will transform us into seeds that will sprout and give beautiful fruits. Tools that will heal our souls and restore the legacy of our ancestors. And that's the purpose of "My African Icons."

But why a children book you may also ask?
Because children are our future, they are the next step toward our world's renaissance.

During one of my breaks, while writing this book, I ended up watching a documentary. It was talking about nature - life in the jungle. Showing the life of numerous species of a region in south America. Among these species were Jaguars and ants. And the encounter between both species taught me something amazing. That lesson also reminded me that our ancestors learned through the observation of nature. Animals were usually associated with the Neteru (Primordial Gods) because the ancestors understood that animals had a very unique connection with the universe. They perceived things that we, the human beings, ignored or could not perceive anymore because they came before us and they remained connected to the planet. For example, in Kemet, it was believed that the Ibis, symbol of Djehuty (Thoth) did not drink any spoiled water. So, to make sure that some water was pure, they watched Ibises behaviors toward that water.

In the documentary, there was an encounter between a baby jaguar and busy legionary ants. The baby was very curious about his environment. He was tasting everything around him. It was his way of discovering his world. And at some point, he noticed the legionary ants. For those of you who don't know it, legionary ants are equipped with a dar of a formidable venom.

During that encounter, the speaker said something that really caught my attention.
He said :
"those ants did not hesitate to use their dar, especially when they had to defend the most precious goods after their queen, which was the rising generation, the brood (larvae)."

I had never really thought about it that way. But after that moment, I understood how, in nature, all species were extremely cautious with their offsprings. Even when they faced adversity, they were usually ready to do anything to protect their babies. And among the most important elements of the babies's lives was their education. Because they knew that without education, they could not survive.

This behavior also contrasted with the way they violently rejected their babies when they reached the age to be independent. But this only happened when they made sure that these babies were educated and strong enough to face the wild.

But this book is not only for children. It is also for any adult who wants to learn more about the true history of Africa. Personally, I have discovered a lot through the process of writing it. It has been one of the greatest challenges of my life. I had never done anything like this before. The process was hard and frustrating. I almost went through depression for many months. But every single time I was rereading the stories of these great African icons, something was lighting up within me. Their stories inspired me to keep going and continue the project.

Among the advantages you will get in this book there is the use of original African names that will help you and all the young people reading this book reconnect with our ancestors. I did my best with the sources that were available to me because the destruction has been terrible. We've lost a lot of major information and all we can do now is try to recover with what is available. To try sometimes to read between the lines.

Through this process, many answers came to me. My connection with the ancestors strengthened itself, and now I want you and all the young Kings and Queens who will read this book to benefit from it.

ATTENTION PLEASE

Before we get into this journey, I want you to do something. This action will be our homage to the ancestors. A way to celebrate them and consecrate the next generations. A way to show that now we know who we really are and that we will take care of our children and teach them who they really are. It is our way to break this toxic cycle.

So, if you're on Instagram, Twitter or Facebook, I'd love to see a video or picture of you holding your book /tablet, with your family or any young King or Queen to whom you offered this book, and if you're up to it, make them hold/wear a paper crown! Only if you're comfortable sharing it, of course.

Use the hashtag #MyAfricanIcons, and if you want to make sure I see it and share it on our platforms, also include my name, @mister_imhotep, somewhere in your message.

I look forward to seeing you and these young Kings & Queens. Feel free to click into the hashtag to see other people in the community who are crowning the youth and breaking the cycle too!

CAN A CHILDREN'S BOOK
CHANGE THE WORLD?
NO.
BUT THE YOUNG PEOPLE
WHO READ IT CAN.

  MR IMHOTEP

MR. IMHOTEP
PRESENTS

MY
AFRICAN
ICONS

THE DIVINE WIFE, MOTHER, & KINGMAKER

According to the mythology of Kemet, at the beginning of times, there was God. His name was Untu (Atum), « the complete one ». Untu created himself using his thought and the sheer force of his will. But Untu was alone. So, he decided to create two children, through a metamorphosis of his own being. He magically divided himself without losing anything and created a son named Shu, the air, and a daughter named Tefnut, the Goddess of mist and moisture. Together, Shu and Tefnut were given the task of bringing order to the world. So, they created Geb the Earth and Nut the Sky.

In turn, Geb and Nut divided themselves and created several children. And together, they represented the Neteru (The primordial Gods). Amongst them was Goddess Aïssata, their first daughter. Aïssata was also known as Assata, Aset or later by the Greeks as Isis. She represented the ideal mother and wife. She was considered the patroness of nature and magic. Aïssata was chosen by her brother, the God Usire, who is commonly known as Osiris, to be his partner. Usire was the first king of Kemet, the God of fertility, agriculture, the afterlife, the dead, resurrection, life, and vegetation. Together with Aïssata, they represented the divine African couple. The ancient Africans believed that both were the ones who first reigned and civilized our world.

While her divine husband Usire worked to abolish violence in the lands, teaching the men and women how to fend for themselves and how to practice agriculture, Aïssata worked to establish order and discipline among their subjects. She even taught the women how to grind wheat and weave cotton into clothes. Aïssata was very versatile, and she had a broad understanding of medicine. She taught the men and women how to cure and treat diseases. She established marriage and familiarized men with domestic means of living. Whenever Usire set out for his expedition to share his knowledge of civilization with other parts of the world, Aïssata always took over the power and ruled in Africa.
According to her myth, the world was a paradise where everyone, man and woman, was equal under their reign, food was abundant, and no one suffered any want. But one day,

their brother, the God Setekh (Seth), the God of war, chaos and storms, who was jealous of their union and success, held a banquet for Usire. During that banquet, he brought in a beautiful box and said that whoever could fit in the box perfectly would get to keep it. However, Setekh was cunning, he had measured Usire's body in his sleep and made sure that he was the only one who could fit in the box. Everyone at the feast was allowed to try if they would fit, and when Usire tried to fit in the box, Setekh closed the lid on him as soon as he entered. The box thus became a sarcophagus for Usire.

Setekh flung the sarcophagus in the Hapi river (Nile River) and it drifted far far away.

Aïssata was devastated, but she did not lose hope. She went looking for the sarcophagus, so her husband could have a proper burial. She found it in a tree in Byblos, a city along the Phoenician coast. She took it and brought it back to Kemet, hiding it in a swamp. But Setekh went hunting that night and found the sarcophagus.

Enraged, he split it into fourteen pieces and scattered them all over Kemet to ensure that Aïssata could never find Usire again and offer him proper burial. However, Aïssata's love for Usire couldn't be stopped. She was determined to honor her husband with a proper burial. With the help of her sister Neb-Het (Nephthys), they went looking for these pieces, but could only find thirteen of the fourteen pieces. A fish had swallowed the last one.

So, Aïssata decided to recreate the last piece with the help of Djehuty (Thoth), the God of wisdom, writing, Medu Neter language (hieroglyphics or the words of God), science, magic, art, judgment, and the dead. When all the pieces were gathered and with the aid of Djehuty's magic, she revived her husband Usire. Together, the divine couple conceived Heru (Horus), their son, the first heir to the throne of Kemet.

Aïssata gave birth to Heru at Khemmis, a city located on the Hapi Delta (Nile Delta). Many dangers faced Heru after birth. Aïssata had to flee with her newborn to escape the wrath of Setekh, the murderer of her husband Usire. She protected and raised Heru until he was old enough to face his uncle Setekh. Heru defeated Setekh and thus succeeded his father on the throne of Kemet.

Goddess Aïssata was an important representation of the pharaoh's power.

All pharaohs were depicted as her children. They sat on the throne she provided. They all possessed the "Heru name crest" or "Horus name," the oldest known title of the rulers of Kemet.

That royal name likened each Pharaoh to the God, Heru. It made them rightful sons and successors of Usire the first pharaoh through his divine spouse Goddess Aïssata.

In the art of Kemet, Aïssata was usually portrayed as a black woman wearing a throne on her head. That throne represented the power to rule in Africa. The throne was the symbol of royalty and was put on Aïssata's head because, according to the original African tradition, the right to rule was passed through the African women. This means that to become a King in Africa and sit on the throne of any kingdom, one had to come from the womb of a native African woman, the direct descendants of Goddess Aïssata.

Among all the African Neteru (Gods), Goddess Aïssata became the most influential. In many places, during the period of the new kingdom, Aïssata was even more prominent than her spouse, God Usire. She was seen as the mother of all pharaohs and was often depicted breastfeeding the pharaoh. Even fellow deities were unable to resist her power. But it is safe to say that she represented motherhood and the ancestral African feminine valor.

The cult of Goddess Aïssata grew so popular that her impact and worship transcended the shores of Kemet and Africa. Historians, merchants, and sailors from all over the world carried her worship across the nations. She became known as the star of the sea and a patron divinity of travelers.

The famous star known by the Kemites as Sabati (Sopdet) today known as Sirius, was associated with her.
Sabati means "to remain still" or "to be stable" in the Mandinka language. And Sirius is known for its stability in the sky.

It never moved and that's what makes it a reference for travelers and sailors who used it to find their way at night. The appearance of the star signified the advent of a New Year and Aïssata was likewise considered the Goddess of rebirth, reincarnation, and as a protector of the dead. She was worshipped up to the Christian era. But somewhere in the 6th century, her main temple of worship was converted into a church. She was honored in great festivals held around spring and autumn. Later on, in the temples, she inspired Mary, the mother of Jesus, who replaced Heru the original African divine child.

Usire (Osiris/Ausar)

He was depicted as a black man wearing the Atef crown which combines the Hedjet, the white crown of Upper Kemet, with curly red ostrich feathers on each side of the crown for the Usire cult.

Setekh (Seth)

Setekh was represented as a composite figure, with a canine body, slanting eyes, square-tipped ears, tufted; various animals (including aardvark, antelope, ass, camel, fennec, greyhound, jackal, jerboa, long-snouted mouse, okapi, oryx, & pig) have been suggested as the basis for his form.

Heru (Horus)

Heru was represented as a falcon headed black man whose right eye was the sun or morning star, representing power and quintessence, and whose left eye was the moon or evening star, representing healing. He is wearing the 'pa sekhemty' the double crown, symbol of dominance over the entire territory of Kemet.

Djehuty (Thoth)

Djehuty was usually represented in human form with an ibis's head. He weighed the hearts of the deceased at their judgment and reported the result to the presiding God, Usire, and his fellow judges. Djehuty's sacred animals were the ibis and the baboon.

IEMHETEPU

THE GOD OF MEDICINE

The site of Saqqara in Kemet, with all its amazing buildings and pyramids is known as one of the masterpieces of the ancient world. Its history reveals the most unbelievable events, and it is highly linked to one of the greatest men who ever existed. The African multi-genius Iemhetepu most commonly known as Imhotep. His name, Iemhetepu, means « The one who has come in peace » in the ancient language of Kemet.

Nothing in the origins of Iemhetepu could tell that he would become such a legend in the history of humanity. Little is known about his early life, but we do know that the young Iemhetepu did not belong to any royal family. He was born a commoner. His father Kanofer, was a distinguished architect, and his mother an African woman named Khereduankh. Together they had nine children.

Africa is known as the cradle of civilization and Sciences. So, education was highly developed in ancient Africa, it was part of the people's daily lives. A family was usually dedicated hereditarily to one single discipline. Without family in the profession, it was very difficult for people to enter a profession. One had to be really exceptional to be allowed to cross these borders. And like his father Kanofer, Iemhetepu was primarily an architect. At nine, the young Iemhetepu started his training. He received a liberal education, so far as such was possible in those days. He was trained in the city of Inebou-Hedjou (Memphis), whose main God was Ptah, God of all craftsmen and architects. The perfect place for all apprentices who aspired to become great architects.

And that's how at only 14, and with passion and dedication, our aspiring architect grew up to become an erudite and a versatile scholar. At that early age, his reputation already crossed the borders of the numerous schools in the country. His educators noticed his passion and learning abilities that were above average. And his work ethic and passion convinced them to promote him towards his natural inclinations. The learning of numerous scientific fields at the same time.

The young man had a very promising future and thanks to his seriousness and the guidance of his elders, he was able to accomplish his potential. He became more than a simple architect. He would go on to also be known as an astronomer, a doctor, an engineer, an inventor, a priest, a magician, and the chief doctor to the Pharaoh.

Thus, he became the first known multi-genius recorded in world history.

As you probably noticed it in his titles, Iemhetepu's reputation reached the royal court. At that time, the King of Kemet was Pharaoh Djoser of the third dynasty. The king heard about his accomplishments and invited him to the court. He nominated him as his chief architect. A title of chief of all works of the king. He was in fact the highest ranked commoner in all history. It meant that he was in charge of all the buildings of the King. This nomination made him the first architect in recorded history we know by name.

During Iemhetepu's childhood, most buildings in Kemet were made of sun-baked brick, wood or stone. But when he became an architect, he came up with a new idea. He designed Djoser's Step Pyramid at Saqqara to be made out of cut stone, a more durable weight-bearing material which allowed the structure to be built much higher and last longer. It was a revolution in the world and that innovation shaped the architectural future of Kemet.

That first pyramid began as a mastaba-shaped structure; these Kemetic tombs in the form of a flat-roofed, rectangular structure with inward sloping sides. But Iemhetepu made it grew to have six stepped layers and reach a height of 200 feet. It was the largest building of its time and the first known monumental building in the world.

The Step Pyramid at Saqqara includes a large stairway leading upward. It would have allowed the Pharaoh in the afterlife to climb up (symbolically, at least) toward the sun

Neter (Sun God) Ra, who, in the Kemetic mythology, had climbed down from the sky to create humans.

Because this type of structure was new, Iemhetepu must also have invented tools and equipment to enable its construction. He also wrote about architecture and his writings greatly influenced later generations of the architects of Kemet. Iemhetepu was also an engineer and inventor, and designed and developed  an irrigation system to bring water from the Hapi river (Nile River) to Inebou-Hedjou (Memphis) where the government was located at the time. Later Kemites (the people of Kemet) revered Iemhetepu so much, that they considered him divine.

As we already talked about it, Iemhetepu was an exceptional person. He also established a reputation as a healer that was so great that he was worshipped as a God for the next 3000 years after his demise. Iemhetepu's wit and exceptional gifts singled him out during the early years.

In the early years of civilization in native Africa and in the world, magic and medicine were related. The Kemites had very advanced knowledge of medicine. They understood the principles of blood circulation four thousand years before they were known in Europe. The Kemites could diagnose more than two hundred diseases, performed successful surgeries and made medicines from plants. They also invented most surgery tools we use today. Iemhetepu was especially gifted in these practices and by 500 BC, his fame had grown. In fact, his influence was significant in the development of Greek medicine during the rise of the European civilizations (Ancient Greece and Rome). Renowned emperors like

Claudius and Tiberius had inscriptions praising Iemhetepu on the walls of their temples. The early Roman Christians described him as a healer, giver of rest, and a prince of peace. In Kemet, the great temple of Amani (Amen) at Nesut-Towi (Karnak) houses two relief sculptures of Iemhetepu depicting him as a very humble black African man. A temple is built in his honor on the island in the Hapi river (Nile river) called Swenet (Philae).

Today, most people when thinking about the origins of medicine think about Hippocrates, the greek scholar who is labelled "the father of modern medicine". But it is not true. Iemhetepu is the real father of medicine. Hippocrates who was born many millennia after Iemhetepu, learned his knowledge of medicine in Africa, from the descendants and students of Iemhetepu. Iemhetepu remains undaunted the God of medicine. He was before the era of Hippocrates.

Iemhetepu is ranked amongst the world's most influential people. His work taught and influenced humanity at a higher scale. He was versatile, charismatic, and well learned. No individual of the ancient world has left a deeper impression on history than Iemhetepu.

Iemhetepu's death was not well recorded just like his birth. It was the Persian conquest of Kemet in 525 BCE that reawaken the consciousness of Iemhetepu. He was elevated to the position of full deity, replacing the God Nefertemu in the great triad of Inebou-Hedjou (Memphis), his birth place. He reigns alongside his mythological parents Ptah, the God of all craftsmen and architects, and Sekhmet, the Goddess of war and pestilence.

Iemhetepu is the only non-royal mortal Kemite besides Amani-Hetepu son of Hapu (Amenhotep son of Hapu) of the 18th dynasty to attain the honor of total deification. Iemhetepu will forever be respected as the father of medicine. His knowledge was and still remains a marvel. When you realize that Iemhetepu was just an ordinary man from a lowly background, it opens our minds to the truth that we are capable of becoming the best at whatever we want to do as long as we put our minds to it.

More importantly, if you are good at what you do, Kings will be at your service. There is a power that is innate in every African: the power of greatness through knowledge. So, go learn as much as you can.

Invention of the stethoscope

It is believed that the stethoscope was invented in France in 1816 by René Laennec at the Necker-Enfants Malades Hospital in Paris. But the truth is that it has been invented in Africa, in Kemet by Africans. Many depictions of stethoscopes appear on the walls of Kemet. Proof that it was already used 4,000 years before René Laennec.

Invention of the Step Pyramid

The step pyramid was the earliest type of African pyramid. Iemhetepu influenced many other cultures all over the world. That's why there are also step pyramids in other parts of Africa, in America and even in Asia. Africans influenced the world since the dawn of times. And they still do it today.

Great Pyramid of Giza

The Great Pyramid of Giza has been the tallest man-made structure in the world for thousands of years. Named one of the Seven Wonders of the Ancient World, the Great Pyramid is the oldest and the only work that has survived into modernity.

AMANI-HETEPU III

THE MAGNIFICENT

It was a little around 1400 BC, in the royal palace by the Hapi river (Nile river), when a young woman was giving birth to her first child. It was a boy, a young prince, and the future emperor of Kemet.

The young woman was the wife of a prince. Her name was Mutemwiya, one of the wives of Prince Djehutimesu (Thutmosis), heir to the throne of Kemet and son of Amani-Hetepu II (Amenhotep II) pharaoh (Ruler) of Kemet.

The newly born prince will be called Amani-Hetepu (Amenhotep), meaning « Amani is satisfied » — After his illustrious grandfather, the ruling emperor. His parents wanted to put him under the protection of the God Amani (Amen) who was the main Neter (Manifestation of God) of Kemet at that time.

No one knew it yet, but the birth of this boy was announcing the beginning of the greatest era of prosperity ever known in the history of Kemet.

The young Prince Amani-Hetepu was put to the care of faithful nurses. He received education at the royal palace at Gurob, learning horsemanship, military warfare, and the act of governance under his tutor, Heqarnehe.

In the twenty-sixth year of his reign, pharaoh Amani-Hetepu II died. His death made his son Djehutimesu, father of our young prince, the new pharaoh of Kemet. He took the reign name of Djehutimesu IV.

Prince Amani-Hetepu was the second son of Pharaoh Djehutimesu IV. Thus, he was not the official heir to the throne. But during the seventh year of his father's reign, his elder brother, Amani-mhat (Amenemhat) the official heir to the throne, died.

Pharaoh Djehutimesu IV was devastated. But he had to designate a new heir as the tradition required, so he chose his eight years old son Amani-Hetepu to be his heir.

Just about three years after that event, in the tenth year of his rule, pharaoh Djehutimesu IV also died. It was unexpected and caught everyone off-guard. That event, made the very young Amani-Hetepu who was only twelve at that time, the new pharaoh of Kemet.

However, a twelve years old boy could not rule an empire alone. He had to be guided. Hence, he was put under the caring eye of his mother, Empress Mutemwia. Thanks to her, the young prince found the strength to lead the huge state funeral of his father. And thereafter, he started his first regnal year. That year started on a very sad note but will end on a lighter one. During his coronation, the young Amani-Hetepu took the reign name of Amani-Hetepu III (Amenhotep III). Following that, he met the one who was destined to be his spouse. The young Tiye, a very beautiful, brilliant young girl of his age.

She was the daughter of a very important family from the region of middle Kemet. Her father was a noble and powerful military leader called Yuya and her mother was a priestess named Tuya.

Tiye will be the love of his life. He loved and respected her, not only because she was the wife of his youth, but because he knew how brilliant she was. They would both grow together and lead Kemet into its greatest golden age.

During his reign, wars and conflicts were scarce. There were no necessity of conquest anymore because even before the reign of his grandfather, his great grandfather, Djehutimesu III (Thutmosis III), had made the already powerful African Kingdom of Kemet, an Empire. It stretched at that time from the land of Kaša (KUSH) in inner Africa to Libya and the Asiatic kingdoms of Assyria and Babylon. Controlling all the nations around. His campaigns had made of his descendants, the most powerful men in the world whose sole objective now was to maintain that African supremacy.

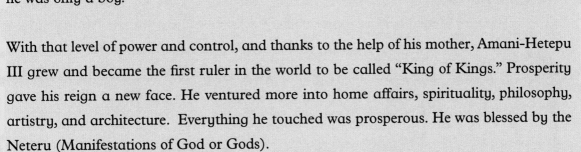

After his grandfather and his father, it was now the turn of the young Amani-Hetepu III to fulfill his ancestors' legacy. The young prince inherited an empire that was already at least 1,600 years old — the most powerful nation in the ancient world — making him the most powerful man in the world. However, he was only a boy.

With that level of power and control, and thanks to the help of his mother, Amani-Hetepu III grew and became the first ruler in the world to be called "King of Kings." Prosperity gave his reign a new face. He ventured more into home affairs, spirituality, philosophy, artistry, and architecture. Everything he touched was prosperous. He was blessed by the Neteru (Manifestations of God or Gods).

He loved his people and wanted to see them prosper. That's why under his rule, women got more rights. African women were already known to possess more rights than any other women in the world at the time. But Amani-Hetepu III went even further. He allowed his Great Royal Spouse, Empress Tiye to function in court and make political decisions. He elevated her at the rank of his equal. Something that had never been seen before in Kemet and did not exist anywhere else, out of Africa. This decision inspired his people and improved the quality of life of women across the empire.

The last twenty-five years of his reign have been a period of great building works and luxury at the court and in arts. The wealth of Kemet came from international trades and an abundant supply of gold from the lands of the Gods, in inner Africa.

Amani-Hetepu III started a style of gigantic buildings that was later copied by pharaoh

Mes-Su-Ra II (Ramesses II). The most popular of all his statues is probably the one known today as the "Colossi of Memnon" built by his great architect called Amani-Hetepu son of Hapu (Amenhotep son of Hapu).

All these buildings, temples, statues, and tombs, still stand the whole world in awe today, millennia after his death. This will earn him the surname of "the Magnificent."

With the power came another level of peace, the magnificent Amani-Hetepu King of Kings relied more on his wisdom to resolve conflicts rather than blood shedding. Being vast in knowledge and wealth, the pharaoh was able to establish diplomatic relations with the kingdoms that surrounded his vast lands. These vassal kings offered their daughters in marriage to him, thus, making him even more powerful, greatly expanding his influence.

Amani-Hetepu will have seven children with his Great Royal Spouse Empress Tiye. They will have two sons, Prince Djehutimesu and Prince Amani-Hetepu; and five daughters, Sitamani (Sitamen), Henuttaneb, Aïssata (Isis), Nebetah, and Beketaten.

Pharaoh Amani-Hetepu and his Great Royal Spouse, Empress Tiye never failed in child upbringing. Even though they lost their eldest son Prince Djehutimesu, they raised their children well and ensured that they understood the family's precepts. Towards the end of his reign, it is believed that the pharaoh made his second son co-regent in order to get him accustomed to the ruling of the empire.

The last years of Amani-Hetepu III's marked the beginning of a religious evolution. An evolution that will be perfected by his son Amani-Hetepu IV. The pharaoh had realized that the Sun, the Aten was the source of all life on this planet. Thus he started to believe that it was the true and unique manifestation of God on earth. With his son, they wanted to make the Aten, the one and only Neter (Manifestation of God) worshipped in Kemet. But they also sought to weaken the influence of the priests of God Amani, the most powerful Neter in Kemet at that time. These priests were becoming extremely influential in the empire.

So, he built two mighty temples for the Aten, the manifestation of God through his solar form. One at Nesut-Towi (Karnak), and he beautified the existing one at Waset (Thebes). His religious reform will be perfected after his death by his son, Amani-Hetepu IV future Khuenaten.

He reigned for almost 40 years and died around his 50's. His Great Royal Spouse, Empress Tiye, lived much long after even up to twelve years. Empress Tiye was a part of the court and an important adviser to Amani-Hetepu III and to their son, the next emperor.

The tale of Amani-Hetepu III illustrates humility that should come with power and wealth, calmness when dealing with issues, wisdom that comes with governance, and creativity that flourishes in artistry. He was the most powerful, yet very humble. He was a good man, an excellent father who played his role in the upbringing of his family. He chaired the emancipation of women. He was highly diplomatic and extremely intelligent. His wisdom was fascinating and the kind of structures that he built during his time showed how vast he was in knowledge. He is one of the wisest men to have lived on earth and controlled perhaps the largest expansion of Kemet in its history. He fulfilled his ancestor's legacy thanks to his wisdom.

Pharaoh Smiting his enemies

Depiction of a Pharaoh wearing the red Crown and smiting with upraised mace his enemies whom he grasps by the forelock. This depiction of the rulers of Kemet originated in the early stages of Kemet, in Kaša. It became an 'icon of majesty' and represented pharaoh's dominance throughout the rest of the history of Kemet and Kaša.

EMPRESS AND GODDESS

he tale of the great Tiye starts around 1400 BC. Hers was a destiny written among the stars. Born into the family of a provincial Kemetic official, in the glorious Empire of Kemet.

Her family came from the city of Khente-Min (Akhmim) in Middle Kemet, between the cities of Khut-en-Aten (Amarna) and Waset (Thebes), the great capital city of Kemet. Her father Yuya, was the royal lieutenant commander of the royal chariot fleet and was also a priest of the local Khente-Min God, Min. Her mother Tuya was a high born woman who was a priestess of the God Min and also an excellent singer.

The young Tiye's family was powerful. Enough to be recognized by the members of the royal family. Her parents were probably really close to Empress Mutemwiya, spouse of the emperor of Kemet at that time. And this detail plays a major role in the realization of Tiye's destiny as we get to find out.

Coming from a noble and well-respected family, Tiye received the best education available in the country at that time. And at the age of 12, her life changed forever. It was during the end of the first regnal year of the new and young Emperor Amani-Hetepu III.

Tiye's family, through the assistance of Empress Mutemwiya (the young emperor's mother), brought her to the palace to become the Great Royal Wife of Amani-Hetepu III, emperor of Kemet, who was also 12 at that time.

The new empress and her husband loved each other at first sight and developed a strong bond through time. Since they knew each other very early in life, they shared similar values, thus making their relationship very special. They were made for each other. These facts had a huge influence on the way they ruled their empire.

The young empress grew to become one of the most influential empresses and queens in the world, giving birth to seven children; from which she had two sons, Djehutimesu (Thutmosis), and Amani-Hetepu (Amenhotep); and five daughters; Sitamani (Sitamen), Henuttaneb, Aïssata (Isis), Nebetah, and Beketaten. Sadly, her son Djehutimesu who was the eldest male child and heir to the throne of her husband died before his parents.

This event led to the pronouncement of her second son, Amani-Hetepu, as the new heir to the throne.

Tiye is the first known empress or queen of Kemet whose name appeared in official declarations, thus making her a key figure in the royal court. The roles and activities she played in the court were only designed for male rulers.

She took an active role in politics and corresponded on her own behalf with foreign dignitaries who clearly respected her wise counsel, intelligence and self-confidence. Proof that they considered her as their equal.

She is believed to have been an adviser of both Amani-Hetepu III her husband, the pharaoh, and Amani-Hetepu IV (Khuenaten; Akhenaten) her son, who is renowned  as one of the most distinctive pharaohs in human history. Whenever the Pharaoh was occupied and unavailable, she took charge of the affairs of the empire.

Tiye was featured prominently on the monuments of Kemet, and seem to have held more power than the empresses and queens who came before her. Her name was even written in cartouches, an honor that was only reserved for official rulers who were usually men. The great number of surviving representations of the empress indicate her great importance to her husband. Empress Tiye is an Olympian figure, and she was indeed larger than the title of empress, queen or wife to the pharaoh. She was much more. She provided the female element that brought vital balance to Amani-Hetepu III's role as pharaoh. And the numerous accomplishment dedicated to her, prove that the emperor was aware of it.

Tiye became so important that she was elevated to the rank of Goddess, a title that only a few queens in the history of Kemet reached. She was the Pharaoh's partner in matters related to both the divine and mortal aspect. She effortlessly flourished in all realms.

Empress Tiye is believed to had died in the eve of 1338 BC. She was originally buried in the Royal Tomb at Khut-en-Aten (Amarna) alongside her son Khuenaten (former Amani-Hetepu IV) and her granddaughter, Meketaten.

During her reign as Great Royal Wife of Amani-Hetepu III, Kemet experienced the greatest golden age period of its history. Her husband is seen as one of the most powerful, if not the most powerful Pharaoh that ruled Kemet. Even her son, who did exploits while he was the pharaoh, had some of his achievements attributed to his mother, Tiye. In fact, her death is seen by some as a contributing factor to Amani-Hetepu IV's (Khuenaten) seeming loss of that his grief over the loss of his mother influenced his total withdrawal.

Tiye's impact on Kemet shows that she was probably the most powerful Great Royal Wife in the history of Kemet, and one of the greatest empresses and queens in World history.

Empress Tiye's story perfectly depicts the power of African women. She was a leader, a queen, an empress, a wife and a mother. Her wise counsel and unparalleled intelligence shows that women are born intelligent, confident, and brave. She seamlessly shows that a woman can be many things and still excel in them all. She and her husband perfectly exemplify what a family should be one that is built on love and understanding. She has been an inspiration for many queens after her, and we should also follow her precepts.

KHUENATEN

THE REVOLUTIONARY

It was a sunny day in Kemet, prince Amani-Hetepu (Amenhotep) grabbed another scroll of papyrus. It was the fifth one that day, but he could not stop reading. He had spent the whole week in that room and had asked the priests of Waset (Thebes) to bring him all the papyruses concerning the Gods of his ancestors. These African Gods, who were worshipped by his people for millennia, and who came from the interior of Africa. He was about to grab the sixth one when four of the pharaoh's elite guards, the famous Medjay's, broke into his room, screaming.

'Majesty! Majesty! The pharaoh needs you right now! It is urgent !'
'Why?" The prince asked, inevitably shocked by his sudden visitors.
He was but just pharaoh's second son and knew that all important queries were always forwarded to his elder brother Djehutimesu (Thutmosis), which is why he had more time to focus on his research and reading.

"We can't tell you right now," they replied. "Your father will explain everything when you meet him. We are merely here as escorts, your Majesty."

"If my father has sent his most important men to escort me, it must mean that this matter is of the utmost importance!" he thought to himself.
Without hesitation, he grabbed his royal pendant and followed them.
It was the early fourteenth century BC, the Empire of Kemet was experiencing its greatest golden age. The country was ruled by one who will be remembered as its most powerful pharaoh, Amani-Hetepu III (Amenhotep III), the prince's father. The most powerful king in the history of Kemet. He ruled using his wisdom, choosing diplomacy over conflict.
He maintained the stability and unity of the Empire of Kemet, whose territory, at that time, stretched from the lands of Kaša (Kush) deep within Africa to the Euphrates and Tiger rivers in Mesopotamia.

That day, the prince discovered that his elder brother, prince Djehutimesu, heir to the throne of Kemet, had passed away. His father grabbed him by his shoulders and looked at him straight in the eyes. The prince's blood pounded in his ears. His father had never looked at him that way before.

"My son," he said, "today, your brother joined the Neteru in the afterlife. May Amani bless him. But now, when it will be my turn to join them, you will be the next pharaoh of Kemet."

He gripped his shoulders a little tighter and said, "this is a great responsibility. You are the heir to my throne now, and you are responsible for our people. You must start your training now."

And as expected, that sad day happened. It was during his 39th regnal year, Amani-Hetepu III died, leaving his throne to his son with the same name, prince Amani-Hetepu. Following his father, the new pharaoh took the reign name of Amani-Hetepu IV and became the new ruler of that vast empire.

At that time, the people of Kemet worshipped Amani (Amen). Amani was the patron God of Waset (Thebes), the capital city of the Empire. He was considered the king of all Neteru (Primordial Gods). The pharaohs who had expelled the Asiatic kings who had invaded the north of Kemet (Lower Kemet) centuries before and who had founded the dynasty to which Amani-Hetepu IV belonged, also came from Waset (Thebes). That's why most pharaohs of that dynasty carried the name of Amani in their own names. They all recognized that all this was possible, thanks to the patronage of the God Amani, savior of Kemet. So, Amani was powerful and irreplaceable to the people of Kemet. On the other hand, there was another God named the Aten. He was the manifestation of God (Untu) through his solar form. He took the aspect of a solar disk, but he was just a minor Neter (God). During the end of his father's life, the old pharaoh had recognized

the growing power of the priesthood of the God Amani, who was becoming almost as influential as the pharaohs. They possessed many lands and could interfere in the royal decisions. Before his death, the old emperor advised his son to find a solution to curb their influence and reinforce the royal family's power in the empire.

And Amani-Hetepu IV followed his father's advice. He decided to elevate the Aten to the rank of most important Neter (God) in the empire instead of Amani. By doing that, he was weakening the influence of the priesthood of Amani. During his studies and with the guidance of his father, Amani-Hetepu IV understood that the Sun was the provider of life on earth.

Thus, he believed that God (Untu, Atum), the giver of life, manifested himself for the most part through the Sun. So, there was only one God, creator of everything, and his name was the Aten.

The pharaoh even announced that the Aten was his father. Making him the only connection between people and God. He became the high priest of his own religion replacing the former priesthood of Amani as intermediate between God and human beings. He had just made it absolutely clear that all religious, military, and political power existed in one man only, and it was him. He had fulfilled his father's wish.

The priesthood of Amani was now useless and powerless. They decided to rebel against those measures and as a response to these rebellious acts, the pharaoh removed all statues and inscriptions of Amani as well as those of all other Neteru (Primordial Gods) and closed their temples across the empire. And to convert his people, he started erecting temples dedicated to the Aten at Nesut-Towi (Karnak) in Waset the capital city. A site that had previously been dedicated to Amani. During his fifth regnal year, he declared the God Aten as the supreme God of Kemet. Now, all his people had to follow the Aten. By reuniting all the Neteru (Primordial Gods) under one single name, Amani-Hetepu IV had just invented what modern scholars called monotheism, the belief that there is only one God. But the Kemites were not really polytheists (believers in the existence of many Gods), because all the Neteru (Primordial Gods) were manifestations or parts of the original and unique God Untu (Atum).

The same year, he changed his name. From his birth, the emperor was known as Amani-Hetepu which means "Amani is content." But since the name of Amani, the fallen God appeared in it, he had to change it. He then became Khuenaten (Akhenaten) which means "Beneficial to the Aten."

Emperor Khuenaten began the construction of a new capital city named Khut-en-Aten (Amarna) which means "Horizon of the Aten". It was located in the middle of Kemet and was supposed to replace Waset (Thebes), city historically known as homeland of Amani and Inebou-Hedjou (Memphis) as the religious focus of the empire. He needed a land that had never worshipped another Neter (God), to worship the Aten.

And this was only the beginning of his revolution. The emperor also decided to change the art of Kemet. Traditionally in Kemet, art was controlled with artistic conventions. This means that artists were not free to do whatever they wanted. They had to depict the world in a beautiful but rigid style defined by their predecessors thousands of years ago. Khuenaten changed that. He asked the court sculptors to represent what they saw and break with the traditional style. The result was a realism that broke away from the rigidity of earlier depictions. That style will later be called the "Khut-en-Aten art" (Amarna art). Individuals such as the emperor, his wife and the young princes and princesses were depicted with elongated skulls and full lips. Features that are very common among the people living in black Africa today.

During that period, civil and military authority was also under the hands of Khuenaten. But the emperor did not care much about it. He preferred spending his time worshipping the Aten, leaving it under the hands of two strong characters: Aya, Khuenaten's father-in-law), who held the title "Father of the God" and the general Horemheb (also Aya's son-in-law). This redoubtable pair of closely related high officials kept everything under control in a discreet manner while Khuenaten was focused on worshipping the Aten.

This period in the Kemetic history is known as the Khut-en-Aten period (Amarna period). Khuenaten had a great respect for women partly because of his upbringing. But also because he saw women as the most important people in the nation. He honored his wife Empress Nefertiti, the same way his father did with his mother. With her he had four daughters; Meritaten, Meketaten, Ankhesenamun, Neferneferuaten, Neferneferure and Sotepenre. He will also have a boy, Tutankhaten with another queen.

Empress Nefertiti and Khuenaten's mother, Empress Tiye, played important roles in his administration. Nefertiti followed her mother-in-law's steps and became an unusually prominent figure in Kemet.

In the long run, Khuenaten's obsession with his spirituality ended up weakening the empire. His lack of interest in the matters of state led to the loss of foreign territories, all while his reforms drained the economy. Consolidating religious, political, and cultural power backfired. Closing the temples of Amani, the most popular Neter (Primordial God) in the empire cut off huge streams of revenue those temples generated for the state. This lead to unprecedented levels of corruption in the country. After a dynamic reign of over seventeen years. Pharaoh Khuenaten died in 1334 BC and was succeeded by Smenkhkare, probably his younger brother. His final resting place remains a mystery because there were records of the disappearance of the emperor's body as well as those of his immediate family. The royal resting place he was constructing for himself at the eastern part of the city of Khut-en-Aten was never completed. Worse off, there are certain historians that record that the remains of Khuenaten were buried twice. First, at Khut-en-Aten, then at Waset, the initial burial ground of all pharaohs in Upper Kemet.

KING PA ANKHY

THE INDESTRUCTIBLE

The name Kaša, Kuši, or Kush characterized the land located right in the south of Kemet. It was also known as Ta-Seti (land of the bow), Nubia (land of gold) and also as Ancient Ethiopia by the Greeks which means "country of the people with burnt faces". Today, it comprises the countries called Sudan and South Sudan. Kaša was the ancestral land of the Kemetic traditions. It was the land of their Gods and ancestors. The Kemites even believed that their God Amani (Amen) lived in the mountain of Gebel Barkal, located in the middle of Kaša.

During the age of the Middle Kingdom in Kemet, Kaša was an official territory of Kemet. But since the days of Mes-Su-Ra II (Ramesses II) of the 19th dynasty, the land of Kaša had gone its own way. The people found a new kingdom, with its capital at Napata, independent from Kemet.

A king named Kashka unified the whole territory of Kaša and even controlled the area of Wawat, the northern part of Kaša that was usually under the influence of Kemet. Kashka was a great leader and he was succeeded by his son Pa ankhy, who redefined history. The name Pa ankhy means "O living one!"

Very little is known of Pa ankhy's early life. Most of what we know about him starts after he ascends the throne of his father as the new King of Kaša. At that time, Kemet was going through a breakdown of its sovereignty. The country was divided into many little kingdoms, ruled by independent small governors. And things were getting worse when many immigrants from Asia and Europe started to gain power in the northern part of the country. The original rulers, who lived in the south, were worried to see their beloved country fall under foreign influence.

Since there were no strong influential ruler anymore in Kemet, the priesthood of Amani at Waset (Thebes), who had recovered its influence after the death of Pharaoh Khuenaten, became the unofficial rulers of Kemet. To solve that crisis that was dividing their country, they decided to ask for help from Kaša.

King Pa ankhy who was extremely powerful, accepted to help. His people shared the same origin, and the same spiritual beliefs than those of Kemet. Amani the God of Kemet was also their God. He was worried to see his northern brothers trade their ancestral traditions for barbaric foreign customs; as the foreigners were unwilling to respect the African values of Kemet.

Pa ankhy understood their plea because he was a fervent worshipper of Amani. In 727 BC, Pa ankhy gathered his army, and marched north to restore the supremacy of Amani. He wanted to bring the whole territory under African control again.

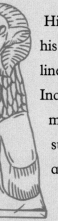

His opponents were a coalition of four "naughty" kings. Pa ankhy in his words referred to them as "naughty children to be brought into line". He quickly defeated them, then treated them with leniency. Inaugurating them as governors. One of those governors; Tefnakht, who maybe of Libyan origin, had other intentions. He was not willing to submit to Pa ankhy. He fled further north into the delta area where he attempted to regroup. But at the same time, he asked for a truce from the King. Pa ankhy who did not know his true intentions, accepted. But Tefnakht never honored the truce. He attacked neighboring cities that were loyal to King Pa ankhy, and allied himself with five governors from the north; Petesis, Osorkon, Pefaabast, Namrut, and Aupot. Together, they wanted Pa ankhy's throne.

Under the guidance of the God Amani, Pa ankhy sent his army to take charge of the emerging crisis. The fleet led by great generals from Kaša defeated the rebels at Khemenu (Hermopolis). But the rebels retreated to the city of Nen-Nesut (Heracleopolis) where they reinforced in anticipation of a second attack which happened very quickly in the area of Sutensenen. They fought on the naval front, then on land.

And Pa ankhy's army achieved a great victory completely rooting out the rebels.

But the rebels did not surrender. They retreated and took refuge in the north, near the city of Khemenu. There, they regrouped and attacked the army of Pa ankhy by surprise. They succeded to recapture governor Namrut's city that had been previously taken.

At the announcement of this news, Pa ankhy decided to leave his capital at Napata in Kaša and do the work himself. He gathered a fresh army and joined his generals at the battlefield. This act of Pa ankhy changed the course of the war greatly. At the sight of their king, the units felt empowered and knew they could not lose anymore.

Pa ankhy moved to the city of Khemenu where the rebels were hidden. He ordered the formation of movable towers to align against the city walls to facilitate the attack. That smart move made the rebels suffer terribly, and within a short while, Namrut surrendered and asked for peace. Pa ankhy accepted and their union was restored.

Pa ankhy continued his triumphant march in the north; and his aura was changing the course of the war. Quickly after, Nen-Nesut, the city of Pefaabast, surrendered.
However, Tefnakht still remained unsubdued in Inebou-Hedjou (Memphis). He had fortified the city, strengthened his army, and mounted up a stronger defense on sea and land.
Pa ankhy was determined, he attacked fiercely. He strategically sailed up the Hapi river (Nile river) to get closer to the city walls and towers on the riverside. He used masts and yards as ladders. He scaled through the fortification and attacked the city. When the governors of Inebou-Hedjou realized he had broken through their defense, they sought to surrender.

Aupot, one of the governors, and Merkaneshu, one of the leaders of the mercenaries, submitted to Pa ankhy. But Tefnakht, the leader of the revolt, and Osorkon, king of Per-Bast (Bubastis), retreated to Iunu (Heliopolis).

Pa ankhy went after them. He was hoping to meet resistance at Iunu and was battle ready. Instead, he was welcomed like a hero. The people chanted his praises calling him "the indestructible". Osorkon and Pelsis surrendered. But Tefnakht retreated beyond the Hapi river (Nile River) in faraway Aradus of Cyprus. There, he grew weary and eventually surrendered himself to Pa ankhy.

Pa ankhy accepted his submission and restored him back to his nome (small kingdom).

A large pink granite block found in 1862 in the temple of Amani at Gebel Barkal (now in Cairo) contained the details of Pa ankhy's conquest. It is called the "Victory Stele".

King Pa ankhy lived the rest of his life victorious and indestructible. He was a hero home and abroad. His descendants make up the mighty 25th dynasty that ruled Kemet for a century. Pa ankhy died in 716 BC. He was buried at El-kuru, north of Gebel Barkal, in the pyramidal field. His name and reputation echoes forever.

The story of Pa ankhy teaches us of the importance of self-control. Pa ankhy was more powerful than his opponents. He could have completely annihilated them. But he always remembered the essential; which was the unity of the people of Africa against the menace coming from foreign lands. His rivals were his African brothers so he forgave them, even though they betrayed him. He knew when to punish but also when to be lenient. He never let his emotions surpass his wisdom. And that ability allowed him to reunify his territory and bring back peace in the Hapi valley (Nile valley).

Representation of Amani in Kaša

In Kaša, God Amani was depicted as a ram-headed, more specifically a woolly ram with curved horns. Amani thus became associated with the ram arising from the aged appearance of the Kaša ram deity, and depictions related to Amani sometimes had small ram's horns, known as the Horns of Amani. Rulers were depicted between his legs as a sign of protection.

Double Iaret or double Uraeus of Kaša

The Iaret is the name of the cobra worn by the Hapi Valley rulers on their brows. The rulers of Kemet wore one cobra on their brows. But when the rulers of Kaša liberated Kemet, they used two Iarets representing their dominance over Kemet and Kaša at the same time. These Kings of the 25th dynasty created by King Pa ankhy were the only rulers in history to have done so. Their empire was larger than those controlled by any other ruler of Kemet.

PRIDE OF KAŠA AND PROTECTOR OF AFRICA

The kingdom of Kaša, Kuši or Kush, in the south of Kemet, was among the most powerful kingdoms of the ancient world. It was also known as Ta-Seti (meaning land of the bow) because of its people who were excellent archers and warriors. More so, it is also called Ethiopia and Nubia, a name derived from the word "nwb" (nub) in the ancient language of Kemet (Medu Neter). It meant gold, and was probably used because of the abundant gold mines located in the region of Kaša.

Still, Kaša will later become known for something else; the high position of its women in their society. In those very ancient times, the Women of Africa already possessed a status comparable to that of modern women. They were respected and venerated since the dawn of time. But those of Kaša reached a level that had never been seen before in world history until today.

It all began centuries after the era of the 25th dynasty founded by pharaoh Pa ankhy of Kaša, around 40 B.C. At that time, Kaša had lost its control over Kemet. The foreigners who instigated crisis in the land of the pharaohs finally succeeded in invading and taking control of it.

Ever since then, a succession of foreign nations occupied and exploited Kemet for about three hundred years; the Libyans from the west, the Assyrians, and Persians from Asia and the Greeks from Europe. Now, it was the turn of the Romans, led by their emperor, Augustus.

Kemet had collapsed and became a small province of the Roman Empire. The Romans were treating the natives as slaves. To avoid that oppression, many of them as well as the last pharaoh, migrated south to join Kaša. The kingdom whose capital was transferred from Napata to the city of Medewi (Meroë) in the south.

There, a series of strong queens started to occupy the throne. They were called Kandake (Candace), a word that may means "Queen Regent" or "Queen Mother" but could also mean "Royal Woman." The word originally referred to "the mother of the king". From around 170 BCE, it was also used to designate a female monarch who reigned independently.

At the time, the Kandake of Kaša was called Amanirenas, also known as Amanirense. According to some scholars, her name means "Amani is her name". Amani (Amen) was the name of the main God of the Kemites (people of Kemet). He was also worshipped by the people Kaša, and most Africans. And just like in Kemet, many Kings of Kaša bore his name in their royal titles. It was a way to show that one was under his protection.

Kandake Amanirenas was not a passive and regular queen. She was a fierce warrior queen. She fought alongside her men during battles and was feared by many.

The Romans who had conquered Kemet were known for their ambitions. They wanted to conquer the world, and Kandake Amanirenas understood that it was only a matter of time before they start invading Kaša. So she had to act quickly.

Since Kemet had fallen, Kaša was the last door that protected inner Africa from the aggression of these foreign powers. Kandake Amanirenas was well aware of this, and would not let it happen. The people of Kaša had never

been invaded by any foreign powers. They were a proud and strong nation. That is why the queen decided to use the element of surprise. She rallied 30,000 soldiers and attacked the Romans in the southern border of Kemet. The Romans tried to defend themselves as well as they could. They possessed a well organized army. During the attack, the ruling Queen lost her husband, King Teriqetas. But with the help of her son Akinidad, heir to the throne of Kaša, they carried on with the rest of the battles. Together, they achieved a great victory; they expanded the territory of Kaša by capturing about two major Roman cities in Kemet (Syene and Philae). They took captives and defaced statues of Emperor Augustus, symbols of the power of Rome in the region. Kandake Amanirenas took the bronze head of a statue of the Roman emperor as her price and hid it in a temple of Kaša dedicated to her victory.

The following year, under the leadership of Roman prefect Gaius Petronius, the Romans tried to recapture Augustus's bronze head in subsequent battles, but they were unsuccessful. Although the loss of his bronze head likeness infuriated the emperor, he could not do anything about it.

At some point, the Romans drove Amanirenas and her warriors out of Syene up to Napata, the ancient capital city of Kaša during the reign of pharaoh Pa ankhy. The Romans had a larger army coming from several countries under their empire. So it was easier for them to carry out reprisal attacks. They launched a devastating attack on Kaša that left Napata in ruins; they even captured some people of Kaša.

During one of the battles, Kandake Amanirenas was injured, and she lost one of her eyes. That's why in some history books, she is called the one-eyed queen of Kaša.
Despite the loss of her eye, the queen was unshaken. The destiny of Africa was in her hands. She remained of high spirits and fought back as many times as she could with her son always by her side. She used terrifying war tactics to show to her enemies that she was not someone to play with.

According to many sources, she fed her Roman captives to lions and also used elephants to attack them. News of her constant attacks and repelling reached Rome, and the situation was becoming very complicated for the Romans who were already dealing with many other battles in different colonies.

So, they decided to negotiate a truce with the Kandake. Amanirenas sent two messengers to Rome to meet with Emperor Augustus. And by 12 BCE, Augustus conceded to Kaša the first cataract, an area that had been occupied by Rome in the southern border of Kemet. The people of Kaša were exempted from paying any tributes to Rome. Something that was exceptional at that time. It meant that Rome had no choice but to respect the strength of Kaša and his Kandake. Augustus and all following Roman emperors became very friendly and extremely cordial to Kaša for the remainder of its existence, which lasted until 350 CE.

Kandake Amanirenas ruled from 40 BC to 10 BC in peace and wellness. Her victory over the Roman Empire and the treaty that was signed in her favor remains one of the golden memories of her lifetime. Queen Amanirenas is perhaps the fearless and most devoted ruler of the kingdom of Kaša. When you realize that she had a smaller army, you would appreciate her bravery the most. She had a strong sense of negotiation and diplomacy. Even the mighty Roman emperors respected her.

Kandake Amanirenas smiting her enemies

Depiction of a Kandake Amanirenas smiting with upraised sword her enemies whom she grasps by the forelock. This pose was first used by the early rulers of Kaša who later created Kemet. It became an 'icon of majesty' and power throughout the rest of the history of Kemet and Kaša, right down to the late period. It expresses Kandake's dominance over her ennemies.

Archery in Ancient Africa

Archery has been invented by Africans. Africans were known as the best archers of the ancient world. The most renown archers were the archers of Kaša. Among the elite units of Kaša, there were the legendary Pitati archers. A contingent of archers who came from Kaša and worked for the pharaoh in Kemet. They were feared and respected for their skills.

QUEEN GUDIT

THE BELLIGERENT QUEEN OF ABYSSINIA

There is very little information on the life that Gudit had as a child. Some facts remain undisputed though. Some of such fact is that she was royalty. A lot of information about her must have been destroyed especially since she was not Christian and that Abyssinia, the territory known as Ethiopia today was and still is a Christian nation.

Gudit grew up in the tenth century, at a time when Christianity was the leading religion in Axum, the major ancient Kingdom of Abyssinia. And even for a little girl born into royalty, belonging to any other religion but Christianity could mean a lot of unfair and even inhuman treatment.

She was the daughter of Maya, king of the Sultanate of Showa, a minor Kingdom in ancient Abyssinia. She was raised in a non-Christian family, and this was probably why she and her family experienced marginalization. Of all things however, Gudit had something going for her; her beauty.

She was a very beautiful girl. Her beauty was so radiant that everywhere she went, people noticed her. It was therefore no surprise that in spite of the social status of non-Christians at that time, a young Christian deacon fell in love with her.

Gudit refused him due to their difference in faith. The young deacon refused to be faced by her refusal. He pursued her with all his affection and passion. In a desperate bid to make him leave her alone, Gudit asked him to do something that she thought would be impossible. Something she thought that he would never be able to do. She asked him to get her a gold pair of shoes and a gold umbrella.

Now though Abyssinia is known for its gold, it wasn't something that a deacon could own or give out just like that. But the young deacon blinded by love, tore off a part of the golden curtain which was donated to the temple by the righteous emperors Abreha and Asbeha. The piece he tore off was equal to the size of Gudit's feet.

Church officials noticed the curtain was torn, they began investigation for three days; they assembled everyone at the square and examined the shoe of each person for three days to check whose foot would fit the torn curtain. Everyone in the city had their feet measured but it did not fit. Gudit was asked to come forward and have her feet examined, it was the exact.

She was arranged for trial immediately.

"The cloth was used to make me a pair of golden shoes." She told them as she narrated the story of her encounter with the deacon.

"Show them to us" they demanded.

She showed them the golden shoes, they examined it and found that they indeed matched the torn robe.

"Why did he do that?" they asked.

No matter what it was that had happened between herself and the young deacon, Gudit felt that she could not get justice because of her spirituality. She was not christian and knew how people like her were treated. But she was not prepared for how the judgment went.

"What can a boy of twenty years do when he sees such beauty?" they started to say.

"She charmed him with her beauty and made him commit this sin!" they claimed.

And it didn't take them a long time to reach the conclusion of the trial and judgment.

The whole case was turned against Gudit. The young deacon was freed of all charges, but Gudit was condemned. They condemned her for making a shoe out of the golden material of the temple. She was first mutilated; they cut her breast with a knife and then condemned her to exile, she was disgraced and chased out of the country up to the boundaries of the Red Sea in Egypt (former Kemet).

There, she was found at the river's bank by Zenobis, the son of the king of Sham in Syria. Shocked by her story, Zenobis decided to heal her wounds then converted her to Judaism, his religion. Later on they got married.

Limited present-day facts of the tenth century, often portrays the era of Gudit as a dark age of Abyssinian history. Why? Because there were internal troubles which continued from the beginning of the tenth century almost till its end, and these activities were arguably motivated by Queen Gudit.

Gudit's marriage to Zenobis heralded the beginning of an era that was going to change the course of events in Abyssinia. She asked her husband to wage war against the kingdom of Axum, where she was mutilated and expelled.

Axum was vast, prosperous and a feared kingdom at that time. It had existed since 100 AD and Zenobis knew that. He doubted the strength of his military to defeat that strong powerful kingdom. However, queen Gudit remained relentless, and so, she decided to send spies to Axum.

When the spies arrived in Axum, they discovered that King Degna Djan of Axum was gone to a battle with his army in Arabia. There, he perished with all his men. That information was above all expectation.

The spies came back very quickly to their queen to announce the great news. Gudit was full of joy. She felt like it was a sign from God, giving her the revenge she had been praying for. She gathered her husband's army and came back to Axum with a thirst for revenge. She first hid in the monastery of Debre Bizen in Eritrea.

Then when they were ready, with her husband as the head of the army, she attacked Axum. They invaded the land when it was most vulnerable. The attack was efficient and swift, Axum's army was already weakened by the loss of several units and of their King. She laid waste to the entire kingdom and border towns especially churches and monasteries, places that symbolized her condemnation and mutilation.

That account of her story that states her royal background, justifies her ascension to the throne after defeating the ruling king of Axum. When she assumed the throne, she began rebuilding, and took diplomatic measures. Several architectural and notable achievements were attributed to her forty year uninterrupted reign.

The somewhat conflicting accounts of her reign resulted into her been identified with different names. She may have been originally named Yodit, which loosely translates as blessed and beautiful. She was later named Gudit to depict her somewhat "evil behavior". She is also known as Judit, and Judith.

In fact, in Amharic language, she is described as "Esato" which loosely translates as "fire." Nothing is recorded as regards as the death of Gudit. But her forty year reign was uninterrupted. She started a new dynasty that lasted for the next 300 years after her death. Some historians records that she was brutal and evil, but still, agreed that she was, if not the most, one of the most powerful ruler and military strategist of Abyssinia before the modern years.

Kingdom of Axum

Axum, also spelled Aksum, was a powerful kingdom in northern Abyssinia (Modern Ethiopia) during the early Christian era. Despite common belief to the contrary, Axum did not originate from one of the Semitic Sabaean kingdoms of southern Arabia but instead developed as a local power. At its apogee (3rd–6th century CE), Axum became the greatest market of northeastern Africa; its merchants traded as far as Alexandria and beyond the Nile River. During the 2nd and 3rd centuries CE its growth as a trading empire increasingly impinged on the power of the kingdom of Meroe (Kaša), the fall of which was brought about in the 4th century by an Axumite invasion. During the 4th century the kings of Axsum were Christianized—thus becoming both politically and religiously linked to Byzantine Egypt (former Kemet).

The Star of David

The Star of David, in Hebrew Magen David ("Shield of David"), Magen also spelled Mogen, is a Jewish symbol composed of two overlaid equilateral triangles that form a six-pointed star. It appears on synagogues, Jewish tombstones, and the flag of the State of Israel. The symbol—which historically was not limited to use by Jews—originated in antiquity, when, side by side with the five-pointed star, it served as a magical sign or as a decoration.

YUSUF BEN TACHFIN

THE MOORISH CONQUEROR

s the sun began to set, the sky above him darkened. A mild wind blew his tagelmust – the veil worn by the Almoravid leaders – he was exhausted. His wielded sword was heavy now, as his silence drowned the victorious chanting of his men.

"Allahu Akbar! Allahu Akbar!" his men chanted, yet he remained still, focused on the horizon. Watching two black-winged kites fighting in the sky, he remembered home – motherland. He did not know it yet, but that very moment would be a turning point in the history of Africa, Europe, and the world. He and his men had upset the chain of the events in world history for the next millennia.

His name was Yusuf Ben Tachfin. Brown in complexion, middle height, thin, little beard, soft voice, black eyes and woolly hair. Yusuf was a Berber, a Moor. He belonged to the Almoravid dynasty, an Islamic group that originated in the desert north of Ghana in what became Upper Senegal in West Africa. They were part of the nomadic Berber-speaking people, regarded as some of the indigenous people of North Africa. At that time, the berbers had been converted to Islam by Arab traders.

At that time, the Almoravids had begun to impose their influence in the north of Africa. The word "Almoravids" derives its meaning from the Qur'an and loosely translates as "leading the jihad (holy war) in the right way". It also refers to the concept of acts of piety, of devotion to the cause of Islam.

Yusuf spent his adulthood at the capital north of the Atlas Mountains.
The movement he identified himself with – the Almoravids, had been divided into two groups. His cousin, Abu Bakr controlled the group to the south, while he controlled the

other faction to the north. Yusuf's rise to prominence was influenced by his cousin Abu Bakr. Abu Bakr was the absolute head of the Almoravids, but left the north to settle some threats among his people down south. While he was away, Yusuf was appointed to act in his stead up north.

After resolving the conflict between Lamtuna and Massufa in the Sahara, Abu Bakr returned to the north to assume his position as the leader of the whole group. But Yusuf had solidified his new position. He had acquired a larger army and possessed more captives. His influence became indisputable. Seeing that, Abu Bakr let things stay the way they were, and returned to the deserts of Sahara indefinitely. Courteously allowing his cousin to rule. However, Yusuf still accorded Abu Bakr all the due respect and never stopped recognizing him as the leader of the Almoravid Empire.

Under the leadership of Yusuf, the Almoravid army had almost conquered the entire territory of Morocco and the western regions of Algeria. His empire was now larger than Western Europe. Cities along the Atlantic had fallen, even Tlemcen and Oran. The Moors, (the coalition of black African muslims who lived in north Africa) controlled the south of Europe.

In Spain, those kings were called Muluk al-tawaif a word that means "kings of the territorial divisions" in Arabic.

Their small kingdoms were threatened by the advancement of European Christians coming from the North and who wanted to fully absorb their kingdoms.

The Moorish leaders not being able to repel the attacks sought for foreign help, and no other was as powerful as the Almoravid at that time, capable of delivering them. So, naturally, they reached out to Yusuf and his Almoravid army. And Yusuf decided to help them. He gathered his army, and got prepared. The fateful date came, the sky was clear and the air was fresh. His fleet crossed the Strait of Gibraltar without resistance, marching through the south of Spain until they reached northeast of Badajoz. There, they met with the Christian resistance – Alfonso VI of Castile with some 2,500 men, including 1,500 cavalries, in which 750 were knights. But unfortunately for the Castilian King, he was outnumbered.

Yusuf knew his advantage. He also knew that his decisions could affect the lives of thousands of people. These men had wives and children at home who were waiting for their return. He decided to exchange messages with Alfonso VI, offering him three choices. To spare the lives of his men, convert to Islam, pay tribute (the jizyah as it was called), or to battle. Alfonso was too proud. He declined all peaceful offers and decided to battle.

It was on Friday 23rd of October 1086. Only a few minutes ago the blackness was absolute. But now the mist was visible, silvery. With the departure of darkness, a growing metallic noise appeared in the distance. Against this backdrop were silhouettes, still as an oil painting and darker than the ravens. Like those infernal birds, the Moors were standing still, waiting for their commanders' signal to collect the souls of those who were going to fall that day.

Yusuf had divided his army into three divisions. The first division was led by Abbad III al-Mu'tamid, the second division was led by himself, and the third division consisted of black African warriors with Talwars (curved swords) and long javelins.

Alfonso launched the attack!

Abbad III al-Mu'tamid and his division responded and battled with Alfonso VI alone till the afternoon. Then Yusuf and his division joined the battle and circled the Castilian King and his troops. At that moment, Alfonso's troops panicked and started to lose ground, then Yusuf ordered the third division of his army to attack and finish the battle.

Half the Castilian army was lost. The dead included counts Rodrigo Muñoz and Vela Oveguez. Two very important members of the Castilian coalition. King Alfonso VI survived, but he sustained an injury to one leg that caused him to limp for the rest of his life.

The battle was a decisive victory for the Almoravids, but the casualties were also heavy on their side. It meant that it was not possible to follow it up, although Yusuf had to return prematurely to Africa due to the death of his heir.

This victory brought an end to Alfonso's expansions. It sent a wave of hope and relief across the Muluk al-tawaif.

A year later, in 1087, Yusuf's cousin Abu Bakr died. That loss made of Yusuf the legitimate ruler of the entire Almoravid Empire. His influence reached a peak never seen before in the region. But in Spain, his victory for the Muluk al-tawaif was short-lived. When Yusuf left, the Christians resumed their attacks. This time, it was with the help of the kings of the small Muslim kingdoms. There was discord among them.

Seeing that, Yusuf intervened again on their behalf and defeated the Christians at the battle of Aledo. But the Muluk al-tawaif never accorded Yusuf, their liberator, the respect he deserved. So, he left and returned to Africa again. But while in Morocco, Yusuf received news of haram (forbidden) and corrupt practices of the Muluk al-tawaif that he had just liberated.

In addition to the fact that they did not honor him for having released them, they dishonored the name of Islam and he could not tolerate that. So, in 1089, he led his army into battle and defeated not just the Christians but conquered the entire small Islamic Kingdoms. He made them his vassals and ruled them all, except for Toledo which remained under the rule of the Christians, and Zaragoza, where he allowed the Banu Hud dynasty to retain its power.

With all the Muslim kingdoms in Spain conquered by the Almoravid army, unity was once again restored. The Almoravid conquests was majorly felt in the north and south, along the east, it only reached a few cities. In Africa, these regions included Algeria and its immediate surroundings. The reason why Yusuf's fleet would not expand its borders is not defined. But the most fitting reason will be that the Almoravids' never wanted to attack cities that shared same values with them. What was most important was peace and unity and not war.

Yusuf died at 101 years old in 1108. His empire started out as a local reform movement among Berbers of the desert, only to grow into a formidable empire. Yusuf restrained fanaticism, and encouraged science which incorporated general learning. His Empire stretched from the Ebro river in Spain up to Senegal. From the most fertile plains of Spain to the mountains of the Sahara desert in Africa.

Civilization started from Africa but Africa was insensitive with what she had. African Kingdoms and Empires were incomparable with Europe in the early years and this is what the life of Yusuf shows us. Africa was well read, advanced, and formidable. People ran to African rulers to deliver them from oppression.

The Tagelmust

A tagelmust (also known as cheich or cheche) is an indigo dyed cotton garment with the appearance of both a veil and a turban. The cloth may exceed ten meters in length.
It is worn mostly by Berber Tuareg men, but is sometimes used by men in other neighbouring ethnic groups, such as the Hausa or Songhai. In recent times, other colors have come into use, with the indigo veils saved for use on special occasions. It usually has many layers that cover the head, and it drapes down to loosely cover the neck.

THE GOLDEN EMPEROR

usa, also known as Mansa Musa, was born in 1280 into a family of rulers. His grand-uncle, the legendary Sundiata Keita, was the founder and conqueror of the great Mandinka dynasty of Kangaba in western Sudan, (modern Mali).

Musa was never an heir to the throne of the Mali Empire. In fact, neither was his father nor grandfather. But extraordinary events led to his ascension to the wealthiest and mightiest throne in Africa at that time.

As a member of the royal family and close to the throne, the young Musa was appointed as deputy to Mansa Abubakari Keita II, the Emperor of Mali at that time. And Musa was the cousin of Abubakari Keita. Emperor Keita was an adventurer and wanted to sail to the end of the great waters (the Atlantic Ocean) and explore the world.

One day, he decided to embark on the journey to explore the Atlantic Ocean but never returned. Some scholars said that he reached the Americas and started a kingdom there. But no one really knows. This unexpected event led to the miraculous ascension of his cousin, Musa, to the throne.

So on the eve of 1324, Musa inherited the richest empire in the world with the most fruitful gold mines known in world history. He became the tenth "Mansa," which translates to "Emperor" of the Mali Empire. His empire spanned from western Sudan, and cuts across the Ghanaian coast, up to the plains of Senegal.

Musa was a Muslim devotee like his predecessors. As customary, in the 17th year of his reign, he embarked on a pilgrimage to Mecca, the holy city of the Islamic religion. This pilgrimage will later become one of the greatest events that occurred in world history. As through it, the world will remember the power and vastness of Africa's wealth.

He began his sojourn from Niani, his capital, to Walata (present-day Oualâta, Mauritania) and on to Tuat (now in Algeria). And then he headed to Cairo in Mameluke Egypt. At that time, Egypt, the former country of the pharaohs that was known as Kemet had fallen under the power of several foreign coalitions.

These invaders came from Europe and the Middle East. The Mamelukes who were also invaders, were slave soldiers, member of one of the armies of slaves that won political control of several kingdoms during the Middle Ages.

And Kemet was one of these kingdoms.

Historians recorded that Mansa Musa had a large entourage, which consisted of 60,000 men and 12,000 servants who carried gold bars. Over 80 camels, which carried 300 pounds of gold dust, while he rode on horseback. Mansa Musa was generous; he gifted people he met along the way to Mecca gold. He even used gold bars as souvenirs.

When he got to Mameluke Egypt, he created a sensation among Cairo's rulers when he refused to bow down before the sultan Al-Malik an-Nasir of the Mamelukes. The Emperor was aware of his rank and knew he was the richest ruler in the world. He could not bow before any other ruler. Yet, he performed many acts of charity and flooded Cairo with gold.

When he reached his destination, he also blessed Mecca with gold. Musa's presence in Egypt, Medina and Mecca caused inflation in the gold market around the world. The prices had to be hiked to measure up with his gold. It was so surreal that the value of gold took over a decade to recover after the emperor's journey in the region.

Mansa Musa did not only excel as an extravagant ruler and a philanthropist, but he was also skilled in matters of war. He expanded his empire almost thrice as much as he inherited and he doubled his army.

While he was returning from pilgrimage, he got the news that his generals had conquered Gao. Gao, also referred to as Gawgaw, was a city in present-day Mali and the capital of the Gao Region. It was located along the river Niger, east-southeast of Timbuktu, the second-largest city after Niani. Gao was ruled by the Songhay people. Their empire was a long time foe. He was so elated he had to journey down to Gao immediately he heard the news.

Mansa Musa was never shy of his achievements; he often joked about the vastness of his empire that it would take a year to travel from one end of his empire to the other.
His journey to Mecca inspired him to learn and invest more in architecture and science. When he returned to Naina, he commenced the construction of schools, universities, and mosques. He employed the services of Abu Ishaq as-Sahill, who was a poet and architect from the city of Granada in Spain.

Mansa Musa transformed the cities of Gao and Timbuktu; he erected new structures and made the cities commercial hubs. The great mosque of Sankore was particularly striking; it became a center for the teaching of Islamic philosophy and law. In more recent times, it evolved into the University of Sankore.

The objective of Mansa Musa was to build libraries and more Islamic universities for everyone to access. He knew that wealth was nothing without knowledge. And that knowledge and wisdom were what made him one of the greatest rulers that walked on earth. These buildings were dynamic and renowned for their splendor and extravagance. They were second to none in Africa and the world. Mansa Musa is believed to be the wealthiest man to ever live on Earth.

Mansa Musa may have died in 1337. He ruled for 25 years. His death is argued to date because even in 1337, he was still active in certain trade decisions. But has never been doubted is the wealth and control that Musa possessed.

In 1375, the map of Africa, prepared by a Spanish mapmaker depicted the emperor of Mali presumably Mansa Musa seated majestically upon a throne holding a golden spectre as traders approached his markets. He became an icon of greatness for Africa. Mansa Musa left a lifelong imprint of Africa's splendour on the world. He ruled in might, and in wit. He was a proud African; he knew who he was and did not bow before any man. He was generous and ready to help people in need. He was a great African ruler who understood that wealth without knowledge was useless.

Mansa Musa's story shows that not only that Africa is the cradle of humanity, of civilization, of science, art and culture, but it is also the wealthiest region in the world. Africans must be proud of their heritage because they have been highly blessed by the Gods.

The crescent moon and star of Islam

Although Islam has no symbol doctrinally associated with it, the symbol of the crescent moon and star (hilal in Arabic) is now widely used to symbolize Islam. This symbol has no religious significance in Islam and Muslims do not hold the crescent and star to be holy or sacred.

Camels in Africa?

Camels are not of African origin. They arrived in Africa with the numerous Asiatic people who settled in the North of the continent. They were introduced around the 3rd century and provided the means for crossing the desert more effectively. In very ancient times Africans used horses and donkeys. Donkeys were the perfect animals to travel across the desert.

QUEEN AMINA

THE GREAT QUEEN OF ZAZZAU

It was a time when West Africa was experiencing major changes. The collapse of the ancient and famous Songhai Empire had left a huge gap in the power structure of the regions of West Africa, and several independent city-states like Zazzau started to rise, trying to fill that gap.

Amina grew up in the ancient Hausa city-state of Zazzau, which is the present day Zaria, a capitol of Kaduna in Nigeria, a country located on the west coast of Africa. Her name, Amina means honest or truthful in the Hausa language.

She was born in 1533 AD and was the granddaughter of Sarkin (king) Zazzau Nohir, the founder of the city-state of Zazzau. Her father was King Nikatau and her mother was Queen Bakwa of Turunku.

The little princess did not have the rosy life of modern princesses. Instead, she was trained very rigorously to become the sovereign of Zazzau.

In 1566, princess Amina lost her father, King Nikatau. It was a terrible moment for the whole family. Her mother, Queen Bakwa, succeeded her husband and became ruler of the Kingdom of Zazzau. The reign of the new queen brought in a lot of reforms and structures to the city state of Zazzau. In fact, queen Bakwa was responsible for major advancements in the city; she ruled wisely and focused mainly on internal issues.

Born in Zazzau, and even though she was a woman, Amina was a recognized heir to the throne by way of her lineage. And because of that, she was trained in horsemanship, military warfare and the art of governance. Skills that all people of royal descent had to master. The young princess even fought in several battles along with her brother, Karama.

After the death of her mother, Karama, Amina's brother took over the reins of government. Amina was already involved in the ruling assemblies as she was the Royal Girl and subsequent Royal Mother being the eldest girl in the royal family.

But in 1576, her brother, King Karama, died. And before his death, Amina had already sealed her place as a warring princess in the kingdom. Everybody knew her strong temper and courage. She was 43 years old when she began her campaign as the ruling queen of Zazzau.

Zazzau was already well established as a powerful kingdom before her ascension to the throne. It was the most pronounced amongst the original seven Hausa states in west Africa. Barely three months after being crowned queen, Amina started a 34 year campaign against neighboring cities in a bid to expand the territory of her kingdom.

Rather than the diplomatic approach of her mother, she was more aggressive. She wanted to rule as a warrior queen who rode at the forefront of her armies. She increased the military might of Zazzau and expanded the territory of the kingdom. She rode from conquest to conquest, vanquishing every kingdom in her path and totally transforming Zazzau from a city-state into an Empire that stretched across the vast territory of Northern Nigeria and down south towards the mouth of the great Niger River.

These conquests brought new opportunities to the newly formed empire of the queen. It opened new trade routes, and many kings had to pay tribute and taxes to Zazzau, which ultimately meant great wealth for Zazzau and its mighty Queen.

Amina was more than a warrior; she was also an innovator. Her desire to keep her people safe led her to introduce "wall building" to her region. With great power and might, she began the fortification of her territories. These fortifications are today known as the "Amina's walls" (Ganwar Amina). She built high walls of mud around her camps and the city of Zazzau.

She doubled her military might, riding from battle to battle until her territory stretched across the vast land of northern Nigeria.

There is a continued disagreement over the actual birth and death of the great Amina of Zaria. What is certain is that she reigned for 34 years. According to the nineteenth-century Muslim scholar, Dan Tafa, she may have died in battle near Bida, in a place known as Attaagar. This area is closer to the present-day Benue State in Nigeria.

The acts of Queen Amina and how bravely she ruled is a motivation for every African child. Amina was everything that she needed to be to keep her kingdom prosperous and secured. Her people loved her and followed her lead not because she was of royal ancestry, but because they respected her values.

WARRIOR QUEEN OF NDONGO & MATAMBA

In the year 1582, a shrill cry of a newborn echoes along the royal corridors of Kabasa, the capital city of the Ndongo kingdom, a part of the country today known as Angola. That high-pitched noise cuts through the tense atmosphere like a sharp warrior sword and a sweet melody of unanimous ululations and chants filled Queen Kengela ka Nkombe's court.

An aged elder draped in a swanky white garment, all covered in blood exits the room with the source of disruption in her palm. She raises the baby in the air, the cut umbilical cord still around the baby's neck.

Her voice proud, she announced,

> "Ancestors have spoken. Nzinga,
> Nzinga Mbande will be your name, and
> you will grow into a great and powerful woman."

And thus, the story of Nzinga began.

Nzinga's father, Mbande a Ngola , was the ruler of both the kingdoms of Mbundu and Ndongo in Africa. So, she was trained to be the best in everything. Growing up, she preferred rolling in the mud, playing with her brothers rather than staying indoors and partaking in other girly activities. She even surpassed her brothers in the handling of the battle axe, royal emblem of the Ndongo kingdom.

While Nzinga was living her childhood to the fullest, the world was transforming at the other end of the planet. Europeans had discovered ocean sailing. They were now able to explore the world and discover what laid on the other sides of the oceans. So they sailed far away in search of captives to use as labor force but also for a better climate, richer soil, and an abundance of natural resources that did not exist in their homeland. Exploration became a very attractive calling for people who were trying to escape poverty and were ready to risk it all for better opportunities.

When they got to African shores, they opened trade relationships, but, noticing how rich in resources Africa was, out of greed, they started to plan permanent settlements, colonies, and encroachment of native African territories, and thus, a new enemy was born – the Portuguese. They sought to colonize Ndongo and control the people and their resources. These led to a number of wars between Natives and European colonists.

In that time, Princess Nzinga had grown up to become a fearless young warrior and she was in charge of a large section of the military. Gone were the sandcastles and imaginary made enemy that she destroyed with her wooden axe. In their place was a seasoned warrior who stood tall alongside her father, leading an army of fierce men and women against the Portuguese invaders, into victory. Nzinga won battle after battle, but in the long run, as fate would have it, she could not maintain the momentum as her army's spears were hardly a match against the Portuguese's firearms.

During that turbulent phase, Nzinga also lost her father. In that moment of grief, the people of Mbundu and Ndongo put all their hopes into the heir to the throne, Nzinga's brother, Ngola Mbande. Even though he was the King, he felt terrified by his sister's bravery and popularity among their people. He forcibly got her son killed and Nzinga sterilized. Nzinga scared of what her brother might do next, relocated to Matamba a neighboring kingdom.

There, she stayed until her brother needed her help and she could no longer bear to see the plight of her people. So Nzinga agreed to meet and negotiate with Dom João Correia de Sousa, the Portuguese Governor at the time. She was a fierce negotiator, so she was able to reach an agreement with the Portuguese, which entailed the withdrawal of Portuguese troops from Ndongo and recognition of its sovereignty. In return, she agreed to open trade routes to the Portuguese. `

That brave princess did all in her power to make sure that the treaty with the Portuguese was respected. She even converted to Christianity, and was baptized in the city of Luanda and took the name of Dona Anna de Sousa in honor of the Portuguese governor's wife when she was baptized. Unfortunately, the Portuguese never honored the treaty they had with Nzinga; they continued to raid the lands. They held people captive and seized precious stones.

On the eve of 1624, her brother, King Mbande died and since the legitimate heir to the throne, Kaza was still a child, Nzinga took over the throne. She was forty-two, and became the first woman to rule the Ndongo Kingdom. That same year, the Portuguese declared war on the Ndongo kingdom, and they won. So, Nzinga fled again to the kingdom of Matamba.

In Matamba, she reinforced her army and then returned to Ndongo. She confronted the Portuguese and finally defeated them in honor of her country.

But, this lionhearted Queen had to face other brutal battles than war too. The people of Ndongo felt that she was not worthy of the throne just because she was a woman. But she proved them wrong when she led her army into battles and won each time. Her victories sealed her claim to the throne and she ascended to the throne in early 1640.

In 1641, the Dutch, who were working in alliance with the Kingdom of Kongo, seized Luanda, headquarters of the Portuguese. Seeing that, Nzinga decided to send them an embassy and concluded an alliance with them against the Portuguese. She also found allies in some neighboring communities. With their help, she expelled the Portuguese from the region.

But the Portuguese were relentless in their quest to conquer Ndongo. So, to keep an eye on them, the queen asked her sister to infiltrate their army. She had to inform the queen of all their military movements and plans. And with the Dutch on her side, queen Nzinga was able to repel the Portuguese from her land.

Nzinga was a very skilled warrior, and she understood the act of war. She implemented guerrilla warfare tactics and was one of the first to order trenches to be made around her territory, created hidden caves, and stocked up on supplies to prepare her people for a potential long siege. She also made an unusual decree, establishing her kingdom as a safe haven for runaway captives seeking refuge from the European colonists.

Queen Nzinga lost the battle of 1641 to the Portuguese when they arrived with reinforcements. She then retreated to Matamba, helping it to become an outstanding kingdom among the African kingdoms of that time. She died in 1663, aged 81. But unfortunately, after her death, Ndongo completely fell under the power of the Portuguese.

Nzinga, a seasoned warrior, efficient politician, a woman who stood proud in spite of adversity, a ruler worthy of her nation's respect. She was a symbol of African pride and resistance against colonialism, a true epitome of a leader, and a fierce protector of her people.

Leopard Skin Symbolism in Africa

All African cultures regard the leopard as an animal that symbolizes all that is noble, courageous and honorable. From North Africa to the south and since the beginning of times. His skin was used as a symbol of enlightenment in the early African kingdoms. In ancient Kasa & Kemet, only the high ranked people could wear it. Kings, priests and those who had been initiated. It meant that they possessed a secret knowledge and power. It is called ingwe by the Zulus, Ngo by the Kongo people.

As ruling queen, Nzinga had the right to wear the leopard skin. She had been initiated by the priests (Ngangas) and was enlightened. She became the most powerful person in her kingdoms.

COMMANDER AND EMPEROR

On a calm and sunny day during the 15th century, in the great African Empire called Mwene Mutapa, a baby boy was born. His parents named him Changa; Changa Dombo. They did not know it yet, but that baby was going to revolutionize the history of southern Africa.

Till today, many people still debate Changa's lineage. While some scholars believe that he was a son of Matope, ruler of the Mwene Mutapa Empire, others believe that he was the son of one of the rulers of the Torwa kingdom. However, both theories are not far-fetched from each other because the Torwa kings were related to the Mwene Mutapas, rulers of the empire carrying the same name.

Mwene Mutapa was a major empire in Southern Africa, their territory stretched across East Africa up to the South and across the Limpopo River. Today, that territory makes up parts of present day Zimbabwe, Mozambique, and Zambia. The Mutapa territory was full of lush green and fertile lands which was also very rich in many minerals. Many people were attracted to this region because of its numerous gold mines and its rich soil which was perfect for agriculture. The smaller kingdom under the Mutapa Empire paid tributes to the Mutapa rulers who were the highest authority in the empire.

Growing up the young Changa Dombo was a cattle herder like many of his kinsmen. He was in charge of the rulers' cattle. And as a herdsman, Changa grew responsible; he learnt how to coordinate himself, and how to properly manage as many cattle that were under his responsibility. He protected them against the wild animals and led them into pasturelands of Southern Africa. He did not know it yet, but these basic skills would later play a major role in his life.

Sometime in the 1670's, the young Changa started to use the Mutapa cattle herds to attract a following. As he began to gather followers, his power, influence, and wealth grew. And with time, the new leader started to have bigger ambitions.

At this period, the Mwene Mutapa were already weakened due to succession disputes. The golden age of the powerful rulers of the Mwene Mutapa Empire, had long passed and local rulers with influence started to rebel and developed their own armies. Changa, of course, was one of them.

He started hatching a plot to gain more independence from the Mutapa rulers. In order to do so, he started seizing lands in the Northeastern part of the empire; lands that had been traditionally under the control of the Mutapa rulers.

By the 1680's his influence in the North-East became considerable. He had already conquered Torwa and Uteve, two important kingdoms and was now openly rebelling against the Mwene Mutapas, the name given to the rulers of the empire. It became obvious to everybody that his ultimate ambition was to seize power and become the new ruler of the greatest and richest empire in Southern Africa at that time.

But there was another threat to his ultimate ambition.

And this time, it did not come from the native kingdoms of the fertile lands of the Mutapa Empire. It came from foreigners, the Portuguese.

At that time, the Portuguese were involved in the trading of various precious resources within African Kingdoms, especially captives and gold which is the most precious resource in the world and was abundant in the Mutapa territory.

Tired of paying tribute to Mutapa rulers to get the gold, the Portuguese decided to rebel and colonize some parts of the territory of the Mutapa Empire. Unfortunately for them, Changa was determined to defeat all people who tried to invade what he considered his territory even if it meant that he had to face numerous enemies at the same time.

In 1684, the Mwenemutapa Mukombwe, ruler of the Mutapa dynasty, was defeated at the battle of Mutapa Munkombwe by Changa Dombo. That battle was regarded as one of Changa's most prestigious victories because he defeated the rightful ruler of the empire, giving him legitimacy to rule.

His prowess led the people to add the title "Amire" to his name. An Arabic term that means "Commander". So, he became Changamire Dombo meaning:

"Commander Changa Dombo".

The basis of Changamire's military power was his extremely large, well trained and disciplined army – the legendary Rozvi Warriors. A group of highly trained warriors who fought wars with spears, rifles and bows. Most modern historians compare Changa's military organization and hierarchy to that of the famous Roman Empire.

In 1693, Changamire and his mighty Rozvi warriors raided the Portuguese settlement at the "Feira" (a Portuguese fortified trading post in Africa) in the area of Dambarare and he defeated them. The news of Changamire's victory spread like wildfire throughout the Kingdom, immediately almost all the Portuguese left their settlements in the region. But some of them, who had settled at the Manyika decided to stay.

That decision infuriated Changamire who considered it as an insult. And that's why in 1695, he finally attacked the last Portuguese bastion of Manyika and defeated them. That defeat was so traumatic to the Portuguese that they never tried to invade the Mutapa plateau again, at least until the fall of the Changamire dynasty.

The fear developed by the Portuguese appear in their writings about Changamire and his legendary Rozvi warriors. They could not believe that a human being could be that powerful and intelligent.

Even though they possessed superior firearms and were supposed to win, Changamire still defeated them while at the same time he was facing many other forces. To the Portuguese, this was humanly impossible, making Changa an exceptional man.

Changamire's prowess made them assume that he had super powers. They even wrote that he was a wizard, a rainmaker and that he could kill people just by touching their body. This was the kind of effect Changamire left on them.

Changamire Dombo was feared till the day he took his last breath. But he lived long enough to see the full establishment of his purpose – the Rozvi Empire. Rozvi comes from the Shona word "Kurozwa" which means to destroy. Changamire Dombo accomplished a great evolution in his lifetime, from the ashes of the Mutapa Kingdom, he created an empire greater and larger than his predecessors. He died in 1696 of natural causes, but his dynasty will carry on the name Changamire, which lasted for over 400 years.

Leopard Skin Symbolism in Africa

All African cultures regard the leopard as an animal that symbolizes all that is noble, courageous and honorable. From North Africa to the south and since the beginning of times, his skin was used as a symbol of enlightenment.
In southern Africa, the leopard is revered as the king of predators and only those of an elevated social position wear its skin. An induna (chief, in Zulu culture) may only wear a headband made of leopard skin but the King may wear as much as he wishes. Changamire wore it when he became a leader of his clan then ruler of his empire.

Cattle domestication was invented in Africa at least around 6000 B.C. The oldest traces of that practice have been discovered in Sudan, in an area known as Wadi el-arab. Since then, it spread all over Africa.

QUEEN NANDI

MOTHER OF DESTINY

Ndlorukazi Nandi kaBebe eLangeni means "the sweet one". It was the name of a young and beautiful girl who we call Nandi. She was born in the city of Melmoth in 1760, to King Bhebhe of the Langeni clan on the south of Africa. Nandi was a regular young girl who loved life like all the other girls of her age.

But her destiny changed the day she went with her friends to visit relatives near the Babanango Hills, a small town located about 58 kilometers north-west of Melmoth. While with her friends, they encountered a young group of hunters from another nation, the Zulu nation. Among them was prince Senzangakhona, son of the king of the Zulu nation.

Prince Senzangakhona Kajama took interest in Nandi at first sight and after that encounter, young Nandi became pregnant. When she found out that she was pregnant, she decide to inform Senzangakhona Kajama of that news, and the news of her pregnancy finally got to the elders of the Zulu tribe. However, the elders did not want to hear about that. They claimed that she was not pregnant but was suffering from a stomach illness caused by the iShaka beetle (an intestinal beetle).

A few months later, Nandi gave birth to a beautiful baby. A Zulu prince that she decided sarcastically to name "Shaka" to spite Senzangakhona and the Zulu elders who told her earlier that she was not pregnant, but was suffering from iShaka.

After the birth of her child, Nandi and her son were taken to the Zulu people to meet with her new family. But she was not well received. She had given birth outside wedlock and this was by tradition a dishonorable act.

Unfortunately for Nandi, this was the beginning of her struggles.

Even though prince Senzangakhona initially attempted to deny paternity of the young Shaka, he eventually married Nandi. But he placed her in the position of a lowly third wife. This meant that Nandi and her son had no legitimacy to the throne of the Zulu. Nandi suffered great humiliation, rejection, and belittling even from the people of her new family. Women of other tribes, and singers also didn't waste time in belittling her. In spite of all those humiliating circumstances and her son being seen as an illegitimate prince, Nandi loved her son with all her heart.

She intimately referred to Prince Shaka as her "umlilwana" which means, "My little blazing fire".

She never lost hope in life and instead, developed an uncommon level of resilience. The pressure she faced never broke her but instead, it made her stronger. And this was because she had never forgot her origins. She knew that what happened to her did not define her. She would always be Princess and Queen Nandi, no matter what happened.

She did everything she could to instill these values into her son, shaping him into one of the most mentally strong children in the region.

The adversity and hatred they experienced, made Nandi and her son Shaka flee the Zulu Nation. The queen feared for her son's life. They wandered from place to place, never really staying anywhere for too long. But at some point, the family arrived at the Mthethwa Nation.

There, for the first time, the small family was treated with kindness and compassion by the king of the Mthethwas. His name was Diniswago. He offered to teach Shaka how to rule and fight. And from that moment, Queen Nandi encouraged her son to be serious and learn as much as he could from his new tutor. The young prince listened to his loving mother, and followed her advice; Learning with his heart.

Queen Nandi constantly reminded Shaka to always stay brave and face the adversity. She always told him that in spite of the terrible circumstances they were facing, he would one day be one of the greatest kings.

And her wish was granted in 1816 when Shaka after returning to his father's nation, defeated his brother to become the new king of the Zulus.

Shaka loved his mother almost to the point of worship. She became the new king's advisor, thus becoming a force for moderation in Shaka's life and ruling. She always advised him to try to find peaceful solutions before thinking about going to war.

Shaka put her in charge of military kraals and gave her the power to govern whenever he was on campaigns. With her presence next to Shaka, the empire grew leaps and bounds over a period of twelve years, despite a proclamation by most people who had said that Shaka would never rule.

Shaka became one of the most important Kings of Africa. He is recognized and respected all over the world just like his mother had predicted. Shaka held women in high esteem, why won't he? He understood their struggle, power, and resilience.

There was a strong bond between Shaka Zulu and his mother, Queen Nandi. He looked up to her almost like a Goddess. However, on the 10th of October, 1827, Queen Nandi kaBhebhe died of dysentery as later revealed by Donald Morris, an archeologist. Shaka was so hurt that he ordered that no crops should be planted during the following year of mourning, and no milk was to be used. This decision of Shaka Zulu was responsible for the basis of the Zulu diet at some time in history.

Presently on her tomb stone is engraved:

"Princess Nandi Mhlongo, Mother of King Shaka" as agreed by the Mhlongo committee in 2011.

The greatness of King Shaka Zulu cannot be well illustrated without the name of Queen Nandi. She was resolute, and disciplined, and she shaped her son into a great visionary leader that revolutionized African warfare.

Queen Nandi remains a source of inspiration to everyone, using her life to show the important roles woman play in the advancement of the society. Showing that women are at the root of a strong society; women raise children, and the education they give their children determine the future of the nations.

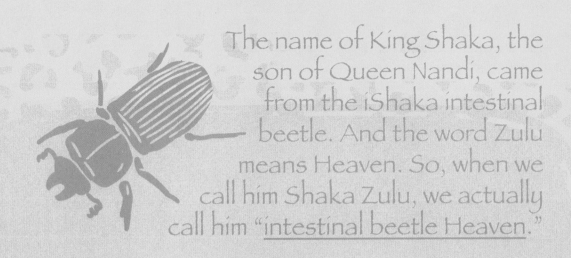

The name of King Shaka, the son of Queen Nandi, came from the iShaka intestinal beetle. And the word Zulu means Heaven. So, when we call him Shaka Zulu, we actually call him "intestinal beetle Heaven."

The Nguni shield

The Nguni shield is a traditional, pointed oval-shaped, ox or cowhide shield which is used by various ethnic groups among the Nguni people of southern Africa. Currently it is used by diviners or for ceremonial and symbolic purposes. It is known as isihlangu, ihawu or ingubha in Zulu, and ikhakaor ikhawu in Xhosa.

THE FIRST GREAT QUEEN OF MADAGASCAR

mong the African icons, Ranavalona I also known as Ramavo is probably one of the most disputed due to her legacy. We know that her story started in the paradisiac African island known today as Madagascar. At that time, the island was known as the Merina Kingdom.

Ramavo was born in 1778, at the royal residence at Ambatomanoina, east of Antananarivo. She was the daughter of Prince Andriantsalamanjaka and Princess Rabodonandriantompo. Her family did not originally belong to the royalty and was not destined to rule at all. But an incredible turnaround led her to the throne of Merina, the largest African island.

It happened when Ramavo was still a young girl. Her father, a brave man, saved the king's life. He alerted King Andrianampoinimerina to an assassination plot planned by his uncle. In return for saving his life, the king adopted his savior's daughter, Ramavo, as his own daughter, which made her officially a princess.

But things even got better for the newly designated princess. The king also decided to give her in marriage to his son and heir to the throne. A prince named Radama.

And as expected, on August 11, 1828, after the king's death, Radama became King Radama I of the kingdom of Merina. Thus, making Ramavo officially the new queen of the Kingdom of Merina.

However, that elevation that looked like a blessing, in a short while, turned out to become a nightmare for the new queen. The other royal wives fostered a lot of hatred and bitterness for her due to her non-royal status. They could not accept the fact that she was granted such great access to what they considered their world. Many of them expected to have that position before the arrival of Ramavo's family. They believed that they deserved it more than her because they truly belonged to the upper classes.

In addition to that unwanted burden that came with her elevation, Queen Ramavo realized that she was not the preferred wife of her husband. And things even got worse, because she bore him no child. Without an heir from her, she risked to completely lose out her privileged position at the death of her husband. Heirs were born to replace old kings.

So it became obvious that all that represents her family's position on the throne of Merina was just her and the king. And if anything should happen to the king, it will automatically mark the end of her family's power, influence and protection.

King Radama died in the summer of 1828. And Queen Ramavo's situation became very bad. A prince named Rakotobe, the eldest son of King Radama's elder sister qualified as the rightful heir to the throne of Merina.

But his position was threatened by the fact that Queen Ramavo was still alive. If she had a child with another man in the future, they would be in position to claim Rakotobe's throne.

This was due to the fact that Queen Ramavo was considered of royal lineage since she had been adopted by the previous king. With her son, they would have a more direct and legitimate right to the throne than him. So, Rakotobe had all the reasons to eliminate the queen, and it would probably happen as soon as he was crowned King of Merina.

Queen Ramavo knew it, but she was convinced that she would be a better leader for her people than Prince Rakotobe, especially because the country was threatened by European nations who were trying to invade the kingdom and enslave her people.

Between the time of her husband's death and the preparations to the installation of the new king, The queen allied herself with powerful officers of the army and the royal court. Together, they decided to try to put her on the throne of Merina. She was more qualified to rule than Rakotobe. But it was very risky attempt because no woman had ever been crowned sovereign of Merina.

With the officials, they decided about the best policy to lead the kingdom. They resolved to promote the traditional practices and African spirituality of Merina.

This was a shift because it opposed to her deceased husband's policy that allowed foreign missionaries into the kingdom to establish their schools. So, they mobilized a group of military men and took over the throne. These very smart moves convinced Rakotobe's supporters to support the new queen instead.

Queen Ramavo took the reign name of Ranavalona I, at her coronation. This name, Ranavalona, means "folded" or "kept aside".

Her rule will be the one of a strong and proud African woman who understood how valuable the ancestral practices were to the survival of the African people. She understood how important it was to keep these ancestral practices in the daily life of her people. And she did everything to keep her kingdom as African cultured as possible. Europeans were using their culture and religion to manipulate other people. It was a strategy used to invade and enslave them slowly. And by remaining focused on their traditional African culture, it made it impossible for the Kingdom of Merina to be invaded. They would not forget who they truly were and wouldn't start thinking they were slaves or inferior.

But her position was very difficult to maintain.

The queen knew that she could not go into a direct confrontation against the Europeans who were highly armed at that time. Thus, she decided to adopt many intelligent measures to fight without creating a major conflict. She restricted the trade activities of foreigners in her kingdom and remained wary of any sort of interaction with white foreigners. Though she did not tolerate foreign influences, she remained open minded and kept learning from everyone, even from the Europeans she fought.

In 1831, she met a French fortune hunter named Jean Laborde and noticed that he was a very intelligent man who knew the Europeans' way of thinking. At that time, communication was not always easy between cultures because Africans followed traditional values that were unknown to Europeans.

Knowing that, the queen decided to use Jean Laborde and his advice to make her kingdom stronger. His knowledge helped her build an arsenal to protect her people. He also helped the queen with very valuable economic advice.

She then went on to suppress and then eradicate western religious teaching and outlawed the teachers and adherents of Christianity. Thanks to those measures, when European nations (France and England) tried to invade and create coups in her kingdom, she successfully repelled all their attempts.

Queen Ranavalona I had a son, Rakoto. Rakoto was officially recognized as the son of King Radama I, her deceased husband even though the king had died more than nine months before the prince's birth. He was likely fathered by a lover of his mother, Andriamihaja, a progressive young officer of the Merina army who the queen may have been tricked into putting to death by conservative ministers at court to erase all pieces of evidence.

Later, when Rakoto became a man, he was influenced by Jean Laborde, the queen's French friend and confidant to turn against her. They conspired to drive her from power. But the queen, however, found out of this plot and saw to it that all the conspirators were punished even though she did not kill all of them. She ruled her kingdom for about forty years and later died in her palace. She was succeeded by her son Rakoto under the regnal name of Radama II.

The life of Queen Ranavalona I is a great example of the value and strength of African women. She was a leader and a visionary who understood that Africans must be proud of their culture and spirituality. That those elements were what made them so strong and special, and they could not follow other people's beliefs. But she accomplished it in keeping her mind opened to the wisdom that could come from foreigners. She will be remembered as one of the greatest heroes of Africa for her courage, wisdom and her dedication for the salvation of her people.

The Vazimba of Madagascar

The first people of the island of Madagascar are known as the Vazimbas. A group of black Africans who settled in the paradisiac island prior to the arrival of all the other groups who later contributed to the great ethnic diversity of the people of that beautiful Island.

MISAKI MIA NIMI

THE ACTIVIST OF KONGO

When the crowd started screaming his name violently, asking Morgan to surrender him to them, Misaki started to expect the worse. His stomach was twisting itself into a giant knot. He remembered that he had trouble getting to sleep the night before, and that earlier that morning, he woke up with a heavy heart. He was pondering if he had made the right decision by not listening to his friends who told him not to leave that day.

After the fall of Kaša (Kush) and Kemet, both of the oldest and greatest African civilizations known today, many Africans from the Hapi valley (Nile Valley) started to migrate within the interior of Africa. They were trying to avoid the violence that was brought by the invaders from Asia. But they did not migrate empty handed. They brought with them a huge population and knowledge that was unknown to many at that time.

Around that same period deep within Africa, many kingdoms started to appear. And these kingdoms used that knowledge, that was at a time only known to the Hapi valley inhabitants. Some of these Kingdoms flourished into great empires while others collapsed due to various reasons. But they were replaced by new ones built from their ashes. Among these new political entities was the Kongo Empire whose headquarters was located in what is today known as the Democratic Republic of Congo, the center of the continent.

Misaki was a prince of Kongo. His full name was Misaki mia Nimi which means « what belongs to me » in the Kikongo language. But he is also known as Dom Nicolau d'Agua Rosada de Sardonia, which is his Portuguese baptismal name. The prince was the son of Henry II, Emperor of Kongo. He was born in the early 1880s, a time when Europeans had discovered ocean sailing. They started sailing all over the world looking for trading partners, resources, captives and fertile lands.

In Africa, Kongo was one of their major trading partners. And the Portuguese who were among the early nations to start sailing in those regions developed a partnership with them.

That friendly relationship developed to the point that the emperor even had an arrangement.with the Portuguese to allow some of his people to be trained in Europe. It was supposed to improve the relationship between both nations. Prince Misaki had been chosen by his father to be trained in Portugal. He was about 15 when he went to Portugal to start his training.

So, in 1845, the young prince arrived in Portugal to study and learn the Portuguese culture. His education in Europe changed his way of living and improved his intelligence and wisdom in a very specific way. That European education, combined with his original African education, made him a very special individual. He could understand both cultures in a way that very few people could at that time.

He was now able to perfectly understand the Portuguese. And he made some horrifying discoveries. The Portuguese were hiding many hideous ambitions in Africa. The continent was rich, and to them, it was the Eldorado, the land of opportunities. They had a strategy while dealing with Africans. They would propose treaties and deals to the kingdoms with no intentions to respect it. Now, they were planning to make Kongo a vassal kingdom. Which means that the Emperor of Kongo would have to obey the orders of the King of Portugal. And that did not make any sense to Misaki, who knew both Kongo and Portugal. He knew how rich and vast his empire was and that Portugal could not rival it. At least both states could be allies. But Kongo could never be a vassal state to Portugal which was at least 20 times smaller than the Kongo Empire.

Experiencing that disrespect towards his people slowly changed Prince Misaki. He was becoming a fervent militant for the independence of Africa. But there was little he could do in fairness because he was not the heir to the throne of Kongo even though he was the son of the King. In Kongo, the throne was claimed in a traditional matrilineal style.

That rule insisted that the king's successor should be the son of his sister. So, Misaki had very little influence in the empire, compared to his cousins.

When he returned to Kongo in 1850, the prince was sent to Luanda, a city in Ndongo, a neighboring kingdom. Ndongo was controlled by the Portuguese at that time. He went there to serve as a senior civil servant. That departure angered many of his people in Kongo. They could not understand why their prince did not want to stay with them. Many felt insulted and thought that Misaki could no longer live with them because he was educated by the Portuguese. That event broke the good relationship that existed between the prince and his people.

In late 1857, the death of his father, King Henry II of Kongo, started an internal conflict among the ruling houses. Two princes were fighting for the throne — both cousins of prince Misaki. There was prince Pedro who was a modernizer and was very close to the Portuguese and his rival, prince Kiambu Ndongo, the brave warrior, also called "Alvaro Dongo" by the Portuguese.

Kiambu Ndongo did not favor any Portuguese connection and was rather allied with the French. Prince Misaki, who at that time was in Lisbon, supported Pedro his rival allied of the Portuguese. But he protested the fact that the Portuguese were intervening in the empire's affairs and trying to influence Pedro. Pedro had to accept a status of vassal of the King of Portugal to have their support.

In 1859, prince Misaki began a series of subtle complains against Portuguese influence in his empire. Misaki wrote several letters of protest. Two of these letters were to individuals. One to Dom Pedro V of Portugal dated September 26, 1859, and one to Dom Pedro II, Emperor of Brazil, with an unknown date. The letters were not acknowledged.

More important than these letters in terms of Misaki's future, however, was a protest letter addressed to a Portuguese daily newspaper. The Jornal do Commercio (Lisbon), December 1, also dated September 26, 1859, and published in Lisbon on December of 1859.

This document became the focus of a cause celebre in Angola

and indirectly resulted in the tragic end of the Prince.

The letter was published on the 1st of December, 1859. It marked the first protest by any African leader against westernization and colonization. It began a new era, a movement completely different from what the world experienced before — an era of African bravery and protest through writing.

In the letter, he stressed that being of royalty and being able to understand the Portuguese made him most suited to be the intermediary between both party.

The major point of Misaki's written protests was that Portugal had no right to claim that the Kongo Empire or Emperor were now "vassals" of Portugal when the truth was that, they were "ancient allies."

During these days, Misaki could not sleep peacefully anymore. He knew now that the Portuguese never had good intentions for his people and that the language barrier was preventing his people to understand that. Unfortunately, when the newspaper publication arrived in Kongo, and Luanda on the 11th of February, 1860, it was completely misunderstood and misinterpreted. The news trickled down to Luanda and caused an uproar.

Some people used it to turn the people against him. They labeled him a traitor working with the Portuguese in order to usurp the throne of Kongo since he was not the official heir. This rumor was not true but the people rather than find out what was true, simply reacted to what they told them.

The Brazilian consul-general in the city warned Prince Misaki that white animosity might endanger his liberty and that he would be wise to escape Luanda. From that point, the young prince started to receive several threats, and his friends advised him to stay where he could be protected, but prince Misaki refused their advice and instead decided to relocate to Brazil and settle there.

Misaki loved his people; he meant no harm; his utmost desire was to liberate them but now they were against him. That morning, he stepped out of his house and started to move towards the Kissembo port in the hope that a Royal Navy Patrol vessel might ferry him to safety. Sadly, on his way to the Kissembo port, he was tailed down by locals led by Prince Kiambu Ndongo who had identified him.

When he reached Kissembo, he entered the house of a British merchant, Mr. Morgan. Morgan's house was soon surrounded by a large group of hostile Africans screaming for the prince. According to one account, Morgan refused to surrender Misaki, and when he raised a British flag to get help, the people broke in, dragged the prince out, and killed him. Another account stated that Misaki succeeded in getting out of the back of the house but was captured. The American commercial agent, Willis, reported that Morgan gave Misaki up after a while, and the crowd then killed him. Misaki was killed after that by his own people. This act sent an awful message to the whole world. For it would mean that Africans enjoyed being colonized.

On another note, it shows the perils of poor communication. Before believing any piece of information and acting upon it, we must always make sure it is true. We must always listen to all the parties involved and make sure their voices are clearly understood before acting. That's how Africans must always proceed with judgement, using wisdom and never letting our emotions take over. Even though he was not the King, Prince Misaki still felt a sense of responsibility and duty to speak for his people. He is an inspiration for all of us to always fight against injustices. His bravery and love for his people will never be forgotten.

Nkisi

In west-central African lore, any object or material substance invested with sacred energy and made available for spiritual protection was called Nkisi.

THE END.

WHO IS YOUR FAVORITE AFRICAN ICON?

Goddess Aïssata

Iemhetepu

Amani-Hetepu III

Empress Tiye

Khuenaten

King Pa ankhy

Kandake Amanirenas

Queen Gudit

Yusuf Ben Tachfin

Mansa Musa

Queen Amina

Nzinga Mbande

Changamire Dombo

Queen Nandi

Ranavalona I

Misaki mia Nimi

FURTHER READING

WEBSITES

mrimhotep.org

brittanica.com

encyclopedia.com

oxfordreference.com

BOOKS

The African origin of civilization (CHEIKH ANTA DIOP)
When we ruled (ROBIN WALKER)
Precolonial Africa (CHEIKH ANTA DIOP)
The destruction of black civilization (CHANCELLOR WILLIAMS)
Black Genesis (ROBERT BAUVAL)
Black Athena (MARTIN BERNAL)
The Golden Age of the Moors (IVAN VAN SERTIMA)
African People in World History (JOHN HENRIK CLARKE)
Niles Valley Contributions to Civilization (ANTHONY BROWDER)
Mots et noms de l'Egype Ancienne (CHABY RICHARD)
The African presence in early Europe (RUNOKO RASHIDI)
Ancient Egypt and Black Africa (THÉOPHILE OBENGA)
Encyclopedia of African History (KEVIN SHILLINGTON)
Dictionary of Ancient Egypt (IAN SHAW AND PAUL NICHOLSON)
The Great Name - Ancient Egyptian Royal Titulary (RONALD J. LEPROHON)
Les Cosmo Theologies Philosophiques de l'Egypte Antique (MUBABINGE BILOLO)
General History of Africa (UNESCO)

SOCIAL MEDIA
Instagram/Twitter: @mister_imhotep
Youtube: Mr. Imhotep
Facebook: Mr. Imhotep

ACKNOWLEDGMENTS

As always, my first thanks go to all our amazing patrons. Your support, love, and patience are greatly appreciated. You stayed with me during all these years no matter what happened. I can only be grateful. I want you to know that you guys, are the true architects behind this book.

I wish to pay special thanks and tribute to:

V. Ashanti, Marie, Kal Mitchell, Thomas Ennis, Ishwiltar, Nelson A. Nobles, Maria Tucker, Marilyn, Lakisha Brown, Ron Mark, Suzie, Jocelyn, Tolu Ay, Louis Banks, See the Dawn, Bibiana S. Ganda, Baboya James, Darren Atkinson, King pharaoh, Diwee Sewell, Kala A. Opusunju, Ragil P., H. Julpikar.

Many others remain unnamed, but they always know my gratitude for their friendship, support and love.
And special thanks to the Montu Team for their amazing support in the completion of this project. **MONTU**

THANK YOU!

⭑ ABOUT THE AUTHOR ⭑

Mr. Imhotep is an independent researcher, artist, designer, author and entrepreneur with a passion for African history. He has been studying African history for over a decade following the paths of great African authors like Cheikh Anta Diop, Ivan Van Sertima, John Henrik Clarke, or Robert Bauval, trying to unveil the true greatness of Africa. He teaches history for over four years with a unique approach that he calls *mindful history*. An approach that focuses on the healing of the people from generational trauma caused by colonization, through the learning of the true African history. The main purpose of that approach is to understand the tricky nature of the history we are being taught and the restoration of the truth by putting each fact in its original context. As he always says, "history has been used to destroy, but history can also be used to heal and build." And that's what he stands for. The healing of the nations through the learning of the true history of Africa. He is the creator of Mr. Imhotep, a platform that gathered over 150 thousand subscribers on several social media platforms like Instagram, Facebook, Youtube and Twitter at the moment this book has been written.

For more info about the author join him here:

@mister_imhotep   mrimhotep.org

★ THE 42 PRINCIPLES OF MA'AT ★

1. I HAVE NOT COMMITTED SIN.
2. I HAVE NOT COMMITTED ROBBERY
   WITH VIOLENCE.
3. I HAVE NOT STOLEN.
4. I HAVE NOT SLAIN MEN AND WOMEN.
5. I HAVE NOT STOLEN GRAIN.
6. I HAVE NOT PURLOINED OFFERINGS.
7. I HAVE NOT STOLEN THE PROPERTY OF THE GODS.
8. I HAVE NOT UTTERED LIES.
9. I HAVE NOT CARRIED AWAY FOOD.
10. I HAVE NOT UTTERED CURSES.
11. I HAVE NOT COMMITTED ADULTERY.
12. I HAVE MADE NONE TO WEEP.
13. I HAVE NOT EATEN THE HEART.
14. I HAVE NOT ATTACKED ANY MAN.
15. I AM NOT A MAN OF DECEIT.
16. I HAVE NOT STOLEN CULTIVATED LAND.
17. I HAVE NOT BEEN AN EAVESDROPPER.
18. I HAVE SLANDERED NO MAN.
19. I HAVE NOT BEEN ANGRY WITHOUT JUST CAUSE.
20. I HAVE NOT DEBAUCHED THE WIFE OF ANY MAN.
21. I HAVE NOT DEBAUCHED THE WIFE OF ANY MAN.
22. I HAVE NOT POLLUTED MYSELF.
23. I HAVE TERRORIZED NONE.
24. I HAVE NOT TRANSGRESSED THE LAW.
25. I HAVE NOT BEEN WROTH.
26. I HAVE NOT SHUT MY EARS TO THE WORDS OF TRUTH.

27. I HAVE NOT BLASPHEMED.
28. I AM NOT A MAN OF VIOLENCE.
29. I AM NOT A STIRRER UP OF STRIFE
    (OR A DISTURBER OF THE PEACE).
30. I HAVE NOT ACTED (OR JUDGED) WITH
    UNDUE HASTE.
31. I HAVE NOT PRIED INTO MATTERS.
32. I HAVE NOT MULTIPLIED MY WORDS IN SPEAKING.
33. I HAVE WRONGED NONE, I HAVE DONE NO EVIL.
34. I HAVE NOT WORKED WITCHCRAFT AGAINST
    THE KING.
35. I HAVE NEVER STOPPED (THE FLOW OF) WATER.
36. I HAVE NEVER RAISED MY VOICE
    (SPOKEN ARROGANTLY, OR IN ANGER).
37. I HAVE NOT CURSED (OR BLASPHEMED) GOD.
38. I HAVE NOT ACTED WITH EVIL RAGE.
39. I HAVE NOT STOLEN THE BREAD OF THE GODS.
40. I HAVE NOT CARRIED AWAY THE KHENFU CAKES
    FROM THE SPIRITS OF THE DEAD.
41. I HAVE NOT SNATCHED AWAY THE BREAD
    OF THE CHILD, NOR TREATED WITH CONTEMPT
    THE GOD OF MY CITY.
42. I HAVE NOT SLAIN THE CATTLE BELONGING
    TO THE GOD.

NOW IT'S YOUR TURN,
TELL ME WHO YOU WILL BECOME...

Made in the USA
Columbia, SC
29 January 2021